the
consul

RALPH RUMNEY

CONVERSATIONS WITH
GÉRARD BERRÉBY
WITH THE HELP OF GIULIO MINGHINI AND CHANTAL OSTERREICHER

TRANSLATED FROM THE FRENCH BY MALCOLM IMRIE

Contributions to the History of the
Situationist International
and Its Time, Vol. II

CITY LIGHTS BOOKS
SAN FRANCISCO

10 9 8 7 6 5 4 3 2 1

Cover and book design: Stefan Gutermuth/doubleu-gee
Editor: James Brook

This work, published as part of the program of aid for publication, received support from the French Ministry of Foreign Affairs and the Cultural Service of the French Embassy in the United States. Cet ouvrage publié dans le cadre du programme d'aide à la publication bénéficie du soutien du Ministère des Affaires Etrangères et du Service Culturel de l'Ambassade de France représenté aux États-Unis.

Library of Congress Cataloging-in-Publication Data

Rumney, Ralph, 1934.
  [Consul. English]
  The consul / by Ralph Rumney ; translated from the French by Malcolm Imrie.
    p. cm. — (Contributions to the history of the Situationist International and its time ; 2)
  ISBN 0-87286-398-0
  1. Rumney, Ralph, 1934—Interviews. 2. Artists—England—Interviews.
3. Internationale situationniste. 4. Avant-garde
(Aesthetics)—Europe—History—20th century. I. Title. II. Series.
  N6797.R83 A35 2002
  700'.92—dc21
                          2002019772

CITY LIGHTS BOOKS are edited by Lawrence Ferlinghetti and Nancy J. Peters and published at the City Lights Bookstore, 261 Columbus Avenue, San Francisco, CA 94133. Visit us on the Web at www.citylights.com.

To Sindbad

Flee the ruins and don't cry in them.
—Marcel Schwob

All individuals, places, and events discussed in these interviews have only a solipsistic existence. Any relation to the realities of anyone else is an unthinkable coincidence.

Do you know what the Greek word *poiesis* means?

It relates to the idea of making.

And *ars*, in Latin?

Practical knowledge.

Yes, and this kind of "making" comes from other Latin authors like Lucretius, who assimilated it into the sphere of art. That definition of art applies just as much to the poet and the artist as it does to the scientist. In my opinion, none of these can exist without the others. Or at least the bringing together of the three activities has been the aim of my work right up to this day. My work has always been based on experiment, in the same way as modern science. And it seems to me very unlikely that I'm ever going to change.

Every art and every investigation, and likewise every practical pursuit or undertaking, seems to aim at some good: hence it has been well said that the Good is that at which all things aim.

ARISTOTLE

So there is no problem with competition, with success or failure, because your career has not been that of a traditional painter or even an avant-garde painter.

I don't believe in avant-gardes. And I've never felt myself to be in competition with other living artists. It doesn't interest me.

There were periods when I sold everything I painted. I don't know where my works have disappeared to. They've been scattered all over the place. That corresponds to a particular way of life, to luck and different circumstances. Things are sold, things are lost. You could almost say that today I'm an artist without works, that they've become accessories.

RALPH RUMNEY
PHOTO: HARRY SHUNK

Marcel Duchamp once said that he had given up paint-ing, and everyone believed him. But it was clear that he had never stopped working.

It would be wrong to think he stopped his own research. Obviously, he needed to give himself some space.

One might have thought that you, too, were a mythical character, dead as a productive artist and as a thinker, but enjoying a certain notoriety for things that were rather legendary, like the famous Guide Psychogéographique de Venise—Psychogeographic Guide to Venice. *But then one discovers that you haven't stopped working, either. To make some sense of all this, let's go right back to the beginning. Where do you come from?*

I was born in Newcastle in 1934. When I was two, we moved to the outskirts of Halifax in Yorkshire. I lived with my parents in an enormous vicarage. There was a huge garden, with an orchard and a vegetable patch—a real asset during the war. I loved that place.

Who were your parents?

My mother was a middle-class Londoner, a doctor's daughter who became a nursing sister and a mis-sionary in Abyssinia. She was proud of being the first white woman admitted to the court of Haile Selassie. A very enlightened woman. Unfortunately, my main memories are of her illness. She died when I was fourteen.

My father was the son of a miner. He started work in the mines when he was twelve and had no formal education. After the war, he took up the study of theology and spent several years in Nyasaland (now

Malawi) as a missionary. Upon his return to England, he took the cloth and became a vicar in Newcastle. It is hard to imagine today the struggle it took then for someone from the working class to make it into the petite bourgeoisie.

Not so far away from the world of Engels . . .

. . . not very far. And Keir Hardie, the great Scottish Marxist Socialist, founder of the Independent Labor Party, the first Labor parliamentary candidate, came to a meeting outside Durham when my father was a child. He warned new recruits to his party: "Watch out—corruption begins with brandy and cigars." Keir Hardie had to share a bed with my father, something of which my father was always proud. My father was a stretcher-bearer in the 1914–18 war—he survived by the skin of his teeth. After the war, he educated himself. He put his trust in the church, to the point of becoming a clergyman.

He read a lot, studied in libraries, things like that. His intellectual development was the result of encounters with various socialist circles. A notion that was at the heart of socialist or laborist movements in England was that you could improve yourself through learning. Some groups had published books to help in this process. They held meetings to spread the theories of Marx and Engels. My father would take me to these meetings when I was just a kid. I heard old workers quoting Hegel.

They'd set up popular universities?

More associations than universities.

Yes, but the popular universities were associations. They were not run by the state. The Communist Party, for example, set some up.

In our case, it wasn't as structured as that. The groups would have a little meeting place, or meetings would simply be held in someone's house. We all got together, and everyone was welcome. Sometimes you'd get a cup of tea or coffee, but during the discussions people took it seriously. I'd never heard of Kant or Engels; I suppose I was more middle class. And I'd see these lads with their dirty hands who'd just come home from the factory and who were debating things like that. That was university for me. Later, in Soho, I found the Malatesta Club, the final redoubt of old English anarchists.

Did you have any other schooling?

Of course. I started with primary school, where I met my first love. I was four or five when I met a little girl. We swore that we would get married when we were grown up. We held hands on afternoon walks. We formed a "crocodile," where you walk in pairs, and we always made sure we were together. I was crazy about her and she was about me. A happy childhood.

When I was about seven my father, deciding that it was necessary for me to have a scholarly, middle-class education, sent me to a private school.

Happiness ended?

Yes. It is a very bad memory.

Tell me more. It sounds terrible.

I was seven. I was very hurt by being separated from my parents and thrown into an unknown world. The school, which had already been damaged by a German naval bombardment in the First World War, had been evacuated from Scarborough to a place called Eshton Hall, not far from Skipton. It was very beautiful. We stayed in a mansion, a real palace, a very elegant edifice built in the early nineteenth century. There must have been seventy pupils in all. It was a society with a strong sense of hierarchy, even between boys only separated by two years. You had to adapt. I was a little bit of a rebel and got angry with the other kids who I thought were accomplices of the system. According to Bertrand Russell, there are three things that derive from Plato: Nazism, communism, and the English education system. It was a kind of torture for me. In the end, I put up with it.

Throughout the war there, my only happy moments were when I found myself alone in the grounds of the mansion, which were quite exten-sive: there was a river, woods, abandoned gardens, orangeries. I loved hunting for birds' nests or tick-ling for trout in the stream. And there were badgers

KNOWLEDGE OF CITIES IS LINKED TO THE DECIPHERING OF THE IMAGES THEY PROFFER AS IF IN A DREAM.
SIEGFRIED KRACAUER
PHOTO: H. SHUNK

A LITTLE MORE PATIENCE AND
ALL WILL END BADLY.
PHOTO: H. SHUNK

and otters. I spent as much time as possible outdoors, in the wild, alone, for it seemed that no one else was interested in those things.

You were different from the other children?

Oh, yes! I think that anyone who has this rebellious side and who manages to keep his creativity quickly finds himself different from others, out of step. Today's educational systems, whether in England, France, or elsewhere, all try to normalize you. It is often very hard to resist, and those who succeed in doing so are rare.

Paradoxically, the English education system is sup-posed to be one of the best.

I'm not very up to date with all that. All I know is that Tony Blair is attacking it, claiming that it must be improved, that it has become archaic, that it doesn't work. Recently, in the United States, it has been shown that in teaching mice to negotiate a labyrinth one can replace electric shocks by an injection of adrenalin. In the same way, one could perhaps use injections instead of corporal punishment in the English education system.

Anyway, the fact is that I spent a certain amount of time within that system and without that I would not be who I am.

At the same time, rebellion was necessary.

When I got out of the system, when I decided to leave school—at sixteen, because I was somewhat precocious—I should have gone on to Oxford. I could write verse in Latin and Greek, something I have since forgotten, thank God. My teachers saw me as a troublemaker, but as rather intelligent. I was quite good in physics, a little less good in the other sciences, very good in English literature and French, or at least relatively so. I still need to correct my mistakes in French.

When did you first come to France?

It was a summer camp outside Briançon, in 1948. I was fourteen. I did a bunk for a few days and got as far as Paris. It was summer; it wasn't cold. I discovered Saint-Germain-des-Prés and, not far from there, the Vert-Galant on the Ile de la Cité, where you could sleep out.

We reached the slippery shore at length,
A haven I but little prized,
For all behind was dark and drear
And all before was night and fear.
How many hours of night or day
In those suspended pangs I lay,
I could not tell; I scarcely knew
If this were human breath I drew.
LORD BYRON, *MAZEPPA*

Did people still swim in the Seine?

Yes, but it wasn't recommended. I caught the first crayfish that I'd ever seen. It had come out of the water and was trying to get back in over the bank. I had no idea what this poor creature was. So I watched it for a while, then put it back in the water. I did a drawing of it.

When did you start drawing?

Like all kids, I think I was always drawing. But the real shock for me in terms of art came a bit later, when I started using libraries. I discovered the Surrealists in a book from around 1936. It was a book on the first Surrealist exhibition in London.

You must have seen reproductions in the catalog.

Yes. It was a book by Herbert Read. In effect, that was where I discovered modern art. The texts also got me into big trouble at school. I wrote an essay where I compared, naively perhaps, Byron's *Mazeppa* with Dalí's *The Great Masturbator*. Naturally, it caused a scandal.

How old were you?

Fifteen, perhaps. It was in the days when they told you that you would go blind if you masturbated. We were surrounded—and we're still surrounded—by a system of power aimed at the suppression of creativity and the control of sexuality.

Throughout my education I was always looking for what was forbidden. Always searching for things that were more or less proscribed. It seemed to me fascinating to note that in books of the nineteenth and early twentieth centuries, whenever there was an "obscene" passage in the translation, they left it in Latin in the text. As I had been taught to read Latin, and since at that age one tends to be rather interested in such things, I had been given the power to discover what I wasn't supposed to know. I had been taught Greek and Latin, but certainly not with that intention. And then in good libraries one could discover works that were much more interesting.

For example?

Lucretius' *De Rerum Natura*. Lucretius is a philosopher who still interests me. I also relished anything that was a bit licentious and the eroticism of classical writers. I read Catullus, Sappho, Ovid, Martial, and Juvenal. And there were also books on art. Through the discovery of the book on Surrealism, I was drawn to seek out the works of the Marquis de Sade.

In the Halifax library, I filled out a slip that was needed in order to get Sade's books. At that time, English law prohibited the reading of such works. If you were an adult and could prove that your research justified consultation of such a book, it was necessary for a representative of the Archbishop of Canterbury to be present while you were reading. He stood behind you and turned the pages.

The librarian knew as little as I did about the Marquis de Sade. When he found out, he shared his discovery with my father, since I was a minor. There was an enormous scandal, and I was generally regarded as a disgusting, perverted brat.

How did your father react?

He went through the roof. I can understand this in one sense: he was a clergyman. He was popular and

GERTRUDE WILLIAMS

Economics of Everyday Life

An examination of the economic issues which directly affect day-to-day life in this country, including the rise and fall of prices, the Dollar Gap, international trade, and the wages question

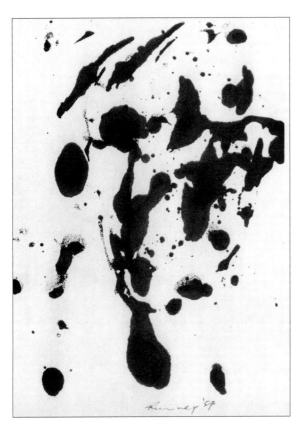

RALPH RUMNEY, *SELF-PORTRAIT*, 1957

respected in his parish. I simply explained to him that I had found Sade's name in a bibliography. It was my father who had taught me how to do research, to use catalogs, to explore different indexes and bibliographies. Moreover, he could sometimes be very open-minded. For example, when he found me painting imaginary nudes, he immediately bought a book on the nude in art, to try to understand. He also gave me Jacob Boehme's *The Signature of All Things*. I read it without understanding very much, not being very mystical at the time, any more than I am now, for that matter. After that, I saved all my money to buy my own books. Within Penguin Books—very cheap paperbacks—there were three series that fascinated me: Penguin Classics, books on art, and Pelicans, focusing on the sciences, in the philosophical sense of the term.

And Marx? How did you come to read him?

In the library. Which led to another report from the librarian to my father, as he had his eye on me by then. But this time my father took my side. Banned books have always intrigued me.

What were your first contacts with the art world?

It was in 1951. I'd hitchhiked to London and arrived there with ten shillings in my pocket. I spent a few days at the Festival of Britain. There I met artists like Philip Martin, Martin Bradley, and Scotty Wilson, all unknown at the time but now enjoying a certain notoriety. Wilson was a kind of Douanier Rousseau, while Martin and Bradley were the leaders of a small group of English artists who took their inspiration from French or Italian art, turning their back on the dominant American culture. They sold their works on the Thames Embankment for a pound each or something like that. It seems crazy and completely inconceivable today. The festival itself was a huge exhibition of art, industry, and music. It was wild! Suddenly removed from my little provincial backwater, I was discovering the modern world. I listened to jazz for the first time. There was also a very important exhibition at the Royal Academy, entitled "The School of Paris 1950." The work which made the greatest impression on me was a painting by Jean Hélion. A funny coincidence, considering what was to happen later. That journey down to London was a real cultural shock for me.

EDWARD THOMPSON

It was hard for you returning to Halifax?

Yes. All the more so because this discovery of the modern world further distanced me from my father. I had the impression that the family ties that bound me to him were unraveling before my eyes. But then I found other families. Communism, first of all. I came to it via Marx and Engels. And I argued with my father.

There was a notorious communist, a man shunned by our village, who lived at the top of the hill behind our house. One day I went to see him. It was the historian Edward Thompson. I said to him: "You are a communist. Like you, I believe that the end justifies the means." There was the proof that I had misunderstood Marx. He told me off for this childish error. I had been raised in a Christian milieu

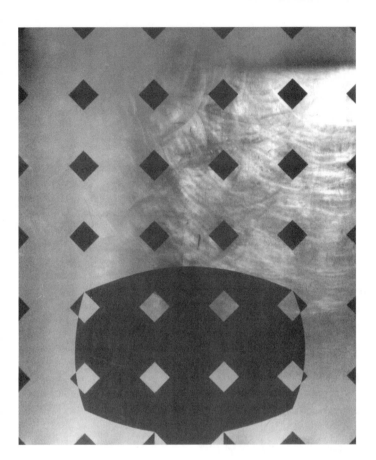

RALPH RUMNEY, *HEAD ON A FLOOR*, 1961

which claimed precisely that the end justified the means. I was sixteen; I wanted to leave the family home and the education system in one go. He found me some little job and, after negotiations with my father, put me up in his house for a while. It was quite an embarrassing situation for my father since Edward Thompson, being a communist, was by this very fact a pariah. In those days Thompson was working for the Workers' Educational Association, the equivalent of the communist universities in France, and was giving lectures in the little villages around Halifax. I learned a great deal from him.

He left the Party after the events in Hungary in
'56. He wrote a monumental, definitive biography
of William Morris and one classic, *The Making of the
English Working Class.*

Did you belong to a communist group yourself?

No, there weren't any in Halifax. I had to create one.
I infiltrated a group of boy and girl scouts from the
Labor Party's Labor League of Youth and won them
over to Marxism. I introduced them to Marx and
brought them into the Young Communist League
with considerable success.

At the same time, I passed the entrance exam for
Oxford. I was given a place as a scholarship student.
But I wanted to go to art school. My father opposed
this. After many arguments, he finally acquiesced,
on condition that I obtained another grant. Which I
managed to do. In the final term I quit my second-
ary school to go to art school.

After a few days, the school phoned my father to
tell him of my absence. Another domestic crisis. In
the end, I stayed at the Halifax School of Art, but
then left after six months because teaching there
was directed towards textile design. My father's
hopes were thus doubly shattered: not only had I
not gone to Oxford, but I had quit art school.

Did you dislike what you were being taught?

The people running the Halifax School of Art came
from the Slade, a London art school known at the
time for its traditionalism. They were excellent
painters, but they lacked any concepts. In the end,
they were just bluffers. We were taught nothing
about color, apart from a book by Oestler on com-
plementary colors and on proscribed color combina-

tions. A dubious theory, because everyone has a different experience of color. I don't know whether I am a great colorist, but, you know, you can always put one color next to any other color because, well, because that's what it's all about.

Artists tend to concentrate on particular colors. With Brauner, it was Indian yellow. Because this was made from the gall bladders of living cows, it was banned because of cruelty to animals and became unobtainable. Brauner was desperate: I gave him a tube that I still had.

Colors can become real obsessions. Matisse was fixated with red throughout his life. With Picasso it was more cyclical—one color per period. I worked for a long time on noncolors: white, black, gold, and silver. The strangest color of all is green. Oestler will tell you that if you mix blue and yellow you will unfailingly get green. But how much blue, how much yellow? You have an infinite number of shades, from pure green, like emerald green, to turquoise, which is more difficult: at what point is it green, and when do you slip over into blue?

In all this there is the question of language. We obviously don't have four million words for the four million colors that you can find on a basic computer. To come back to green, I really don't know what "green" means. I know all the different shades of red or blue, but the range of greens is infinite. It was one of the first mysteries I encountered, the mystery of this endlessly variable mixture of yellow and blue. You can find it here and there in my paintings, but it's a color that I find difficult to handle. And on top of all that, it is said to bring misfortune—not that this makes much difference to me: I find that life brings misfortune.

We can take the example of the Eskimos, who have a great number of words to describe snow, according to its color and its texture. Theirs is a civ-

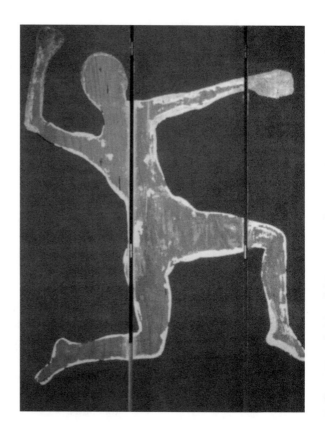

RALPH RUMNEY, *OUTRANCE*

ilization that is highly attentive to the slightest changes of light, which for me means precisely to color. But it is wrong to think, as some people claim, that our own languages do not have so many words. In English and French there are at least a dozen. No color can be fixed or finalized. No two people will perceive it in exactly the same way. And that is something extraordinary, because art is about perception as well as about concepts.

When I send one of my paintings out into the world, it takes on its own life, and I know that it will probably be perceived very differently. Take brown, for example: most people don't see it as a particularly strident color, but there are some brown paintings which really knock me out.

Along with your artistic activities, were you still involved in politics?

Yes. I kept up my involvement with young people in the Labor Party, in the Labor League of Youth. Having become an activist, I gave out tracts until the moment where my differences with the Communist Party were too serious. I got caught up in a little war with the official police of the Communist Party. I gave a speech to the Young Communist League in Bradford. I was supposed to encourage young people to join the army so that they could learn how to fight in preparation for the revolution. But instead, I proclaimed that that was the last thing they should do, because it would mean they were really training to kill our comrades. My speech was very badly received. I was marginalized as a pacifist because I had openly taken a stand against the Korean War. It must be said that the YCL was Stalinist at this time. To avoid being sent to the front, I left for Cornwall. I had to go before a tribunal. In Bath, I tried to get conscientious objector status.

Was conscientious objection legal in England then? Because in France, this came much later.

In theory, yes. But if my arguments weren't persuasive, I could have been sent to prison at Her Majesty's pleasure, theoretically until the age of twenty-seven. At the final appeal hearing I told the judge that I was unable to convince him that I was a conscientious objector, just as I would be unable to convince him that I wasn't a homosexual. My intention was to demonstrate the impossibility of proving a negative. How can you prove that you will not kill another person? Only by going through your life without killing anyone. The head of the tribunal reacted rather violently. Taking my answer as an avowal of homosexuality, he treated me with repugnance. I was the only person not to use a religious alibi to justify my objection. I was told I could carry out my military service in a noncombatant unit—to which I replied, quoting Napoleon, that an army marches on its stomach. Throughout this delicate situation with English justice, I lived in several different places in Cornwall. There's a little fishing village called St. Ives. Nicholson and Barbara Hepworth had moved there in 1939, and at the end of the war this forgotten corner became the center of abstract art in England. Among the painters who worked there were Terry Frost, Patrick Heron (perhaps the most important theorist of the group), and Brian Winter. In the middle of the 1950s, Heron came under the influence of Clement Greenberg, and the group, which benefited from American grants at the time, rapidly degenerated into *artism*. I worked for Barbara for some time. I considered myself then to be an abstract painter. However, for obvious commercial reasons I also painted local landscapes, boats, and so on, in the hope that tourists would buy them—which none of them did, as a matter of fact. But even then I was aware that abstract art and realism were one and the same thing, in the sense that many paintings that are called abstract are considerably more real than so-called realist paintings. For example, I have a weakness for Malevitch. White on white, back to color again. To me, there is a kind of realism there, even though it is apparently one of the least realist canvases imaginable. Abstract means détourned—there's an inherent abstraction in the language of Hieronymus Bosch, the yellow, the blue want to say something. If it is only a matter of painting well and putting colors together, making everything pretty, then it isn't painting anymore, it's a matter of greeting cards.

BARBARA HEPWORTH

Did you stay long in Cornwall?

No, just a few months. I returned to the capital.
London had suffered serious bomb damage in the
war, and there were ruins everywhere. A certain
Buchanan, delegated by the government, had been
put in charge of reconstructing the city. His town
plan was perfectly clear, and it was put into effect:
he wanted to build roads everywhere for all the cars
that would come with the new surge in industry. A
city of traffic jams.

I used to say that he did more damage to London
than the Luftwaffe, a phrase recently repeated by
the Prince of Wales. Pompidou followed Buchanan
in building flyovers and flattening whole quarters,
like the thirteenth, thus turning Paris into the disaster that we know today. Give them nice roads and
the cars will keep on coming, as we all know.

I became aware that none of this was any good in
1952. It was American-style modernization, trying to
turn London into Los Angeles. Everyone loved the
idea. But I wanted a London that would be con-
structed out of pedestrian zones. I would have liked
it to become a grouping together of different dis-
tricts, as it was in the beginning. I thought that main
roads should be built on the periphery of the villages that made up London.

Even if I was unaware that it was being defined in
Paris at the same time, the concept of psychogeography came to me simultaneously. I have often
noticed that when an idea germinates in the minds
of several people who don't know each other, many
are those who will claim paternity.

Being pretentious at the time, I held a meeting at
the Institute of Contemporary Arts in London to
explain how we had to reconstruct London. Once
again, I was unpopular: I proclaimed that Buchanan
was doing a bad job and suggested that at least one

per cent of the budget allocated for the rebuilding should be spent on research among those people who were living in the tower blocks that were becoming more and more a part of the urban fabric, as in Tower Hamlets. I thought that by undertaking this preliminary study, he would obtain a more satisfactory result. My theory of urbanism was a very personal one.

UNITARY URBANISM. Theory of the concomitant use of arts and techniques contributing to the integrated construction of a milieu in dynamic relation to behavioral experience.
INTERNATIONALE SITUATIONNISTE, No. 1

Did Buchanan listen to you?

Far from it. Indeed, no one listened to me. I was seen as a little jerk. I was so much younger than the others. And my plans seemed so mad that no one wanted to follow me and put them into practice.

You had no more problems with military service?

If only! I was summoned for a medical examination. If I attended, it would mean that I accepted the principle. I would have been called up. The only thing to do was not go.

How did you get out of it?

I took my passport and buggered off to Paris. It goes without saying that I hadn't a sou. I discovered material poverty at the same time as intellectual wealth. Drawn to the area like a lover, I spontaneously ended up right in the heart of Saint-Germain-des-Prés, then home to a cult of drinking and thinking. It was there that I encountered the Letterists.

There were certain rites of passage that one had to undergo in order to be accepted into particular cafés, like Moineau's. You had to know what Lautréamont, Rimbaud, Nietzsche, or Hegel thought about such and such, and if you didn't know, you would be told

It is only too true that the world is governed by force and not by wisdom, for those who rule it may be and often are ignorant; thus it is that when a prince protects men of letters, he does it for the sake of vanity or ambition. It is known that ordinary actions become great deeds when recounted by illustrious authors; for this reason, the prince who is not great in himself will seek someone capable of representing him as such.

VITTORIO ALFIERI,
DEL PRINCIPE E DELLE LETTERE

to get lost or at least treated as a complete fool. At first, I felt a bit left out: I only knew school French, and this didn't allow me to join in serious discussions. But one way and another I managed to get myself accepted by some people.

Was your knowledge of alcohol better than that of French?

The two developed in parallel. When I got to Paris, drinking was the only real activity. At the start we were not alcoholics or drunks, but we drank a lot. At the Flore and the Deux Magots there was a kind of intellectual bourgeoisie, of which Sartre was the most notorious representative. They wouldn't get drunk in public. I would drink with my friends to distinguish myself from these kinds of people. When Mendès-France put up posters warning that "alcohol kills slowly," our reaction was more or less political—we wrote underneath: "We're not in a hurry."

Who were your drinking companions?

Everyone one met at Moineau's or in the area—like Guy Debord, Jean-Claude Guilbert, Vali, François Dufrêne, and other individuals encountered by chance, whose names, even faces, I no longer remember. They were part of the background, and I drank with them as I could have drunk with anyone else.

So the cafés were the start of it all. Is that where you met Guy Debord?

Yes, undoubtedly at Moineau's, where you would find him almost every day. Like all the other young men, I was trying to pick up women there. Along with Jean-Claude Guilbert, Debord had one of the sharpest minds I have ever encountered. First, there was his voice, then his language, which was always elegant. Guy had charisma, genius, but he also had a kind of hold, a kind of power, over whatever was going on around him. He was a generous and apparently open man. As I got to know him better, I came to realize that he was a paradoxical figure. He needed to be surrounded by intelligent people, and his charm was magnetic.

Guy was magic, but malicious, too, when he wanted to be. Always delightful and then, from one day to the next, bang, he would shut the door in your face. There you are, that was my first impression.

What did you talk about with Debord?

Being young, we often talked about philosophy. He had more of a head for it than I did. When one spoke of the soviets, the workers' councils, he would say that ideally they represented absolute democracy. Anyway, I think he was already turning over the ideas for *The Society of the Spectacle* at the time. I recently learned of a letter from Guy dating from 1963 in which he said that he was already writing that book, which seems to contradict the official version.

I remember a conversation about the powerlessness of the artist in contemporary society. At the time of Leonardo, Michelangelo, and Giotto, the artist was welcomed at court, and Benvenuto Cellini was a counselor of the prince and the pope. The artist rubbed shoulders with the powerful and was close to those who ruled. I do not approve of popes or princes, but I still think it would be good if the artist could reconquer his place in society. I considered myself to be an artist, and I still do. And I see that as a privileged role to play in society, even if in

THIS

PAPER IS NOT A GARDEN OF LITERATURE

it is a

HOTBED

WE

ARE NOT TRYING TO BE FAMOUS

NOR

are we

TRYING TO REFORM THE WORLD

WE

are trying to

ASSERT THE RIGHT OF THE ARTIST TO BE

CIVILISED

WE

ARE FIGHTING A WAR AGAINST

THE MIDDLE CLASS MIND

IT IS THE PERPETUAL WAR OF THE

ARTIST

VE HAVE NO ASSOCIATION WITH THE READERS DIGEST

What we print now will be bourgeois and passé within twenty years

THIS HAS ALWAYS BEEN THE CASE

GOD BLESS WARDOUR STREET

If you drop the bomb you will find

EUNUCHS

IN THE BOTTOMS OF YOUR BEDS

The whore of Babylon was a damp virgin

OTHER VOICES. VOL. I, MARCH 1955

a sense it excludes me. Some careerist artists, on the contrary, have a fine life out of this, but not me. No doubt I envy them a little and would like to have more money, but I find it hard to see them as better than me. And that goes for the majority of my contemporaries. Instead of building motorways and other rubbish, there might be better things to do: art once played a real role in society, and I thought it might be possible to reproduce that situation. In 1962, Debord didn't believe that at all. He was wrong, I think. In my opinion, the artist lost his influence when he distanced himself from science. The unity of art and science goes back to prehistory. The prehistoric works that we call art today exist on the boundaries of the technology of their times. This unity persisted right up to the Renaissance. Visual cultures and science were linked. The constructions that we find in Florence or Rome were the work of artists who were also architects and engineers. There was no boundary or specialization. It was a total praxis.

Did you have to stay long in France because of the problem of military service?

I returned to London after a year, somewhat apprehensively, but I quickly realized that no one was searching for me very actively, as I was living quite a public life. In 1953, to get myself heard and to acquire a certain legitimacy, I set up a weekly review called *Other Voices*. I was the editor. Stefan Themerson published several pieces in it, as did other English writers like Bernard Kops, Peter Fisk, C.H. Sisson, Hugo Manning, and so on. I even asked Gaston Criel to contribute because I had read *La Grande Foutaise*, which gave a good description of local life at the time, but the text he sent me was unusable.

I have heard that he was a barman in Lille and worked for the radio in Tunisia. And later he was Sartre's secretary for a while.

But who wasn't? Sartre didn't have much luck with his secretaries—think of Jean Cau!

You mentioned Stefan Themerson among those who collaborated on Other Voices.

He was an adorable man. Full of warmth, speaking several languages, a philosopher, a filmmaker. He was in Lodz, at the cinema school there, which still exists. He made a film there which was lost for a long time, entitled *The Adventure of a Good Citizen.* It tells the story of two men struggling to get up a hill carrying a wardrobe. When the USSR swallowed up eastern Poland, the film disappeared.

Much later, Roman Polanski, who had been at the same film school, made *Two Men and a Wardrobe,* which was a plagiarism. Investigations were made. After many difficulties, the Russians provided Stefan with a copy of his film. It must now be in the archives of the Themerson Foundation. When the Germans invaded, he managed to get out of France and came to live in London with his wife Franciszka, a remarkable artist. She was the one who introduced Alfred Jarry into England with an illustrated edition of *Ubu roi.* Stefan set up a publishing house called Gaberbocchus—there is a Dutch publisher today which has republished some of their titles. He was a kind of Dadaist rabbi. Though he was quite close to Bertrand Russell, he had a mind that was almost Talmudic. A continual questioning of hermeneutics and ethics runs through his writing, which often seems like a cheeky but respectful dialogue with Russell.

LETTER FROM THEMERSON TO
RALPH RUMNEY

OTHER VOICES

Vol. 1 No. 6

Friday, March 4th 1955

EDITORIAL

How Low Can You Get ?

In my editorial in the first issue I said that I thought artists should try to popularise their work. This does not mean that one should write down. If artists are so high and mighty that what they write is unintelligible to anyone who approaches their work with an open mind, it is clearly time to try to encourage artists to make their way quietly to South Sea islands. Art is not an intellectual cake-walk.

Let me add one more to the long list of claims to remembrance which this century can offer to the High Court of History. In the XXth century the intellectuals got loose. All you need to do to get a nice advanced job is to be cultured. Put the Reader's Digest under your arm, and walk in looking as if you were a theorist (of course, you probably are).

There are too many people of intellect trying to tell us where we have gone wrong. Well, it's all wrong, in theory. Let us try to write what we feel, not what we think. There is so much thinking going on today, that there is a grave danger of a catalytic chain reaction being set up which would cause the brain of intellectuals in all countries to swell almost as large as those of the politicians who govern them.

Art is a subconscious product. The artist is the man who is able to adjust himself to his intensity by translating it into communicable symbols. Art has a tendency to be humorous, sometimes. Art is nothing whatever to do with beauty. If beauty enters into a work of art this is incidental to its validity as art. It is no more possible to understand a work of art than it is possible to understand language. Words do not mean anything. They create associations in the mind. If these associations happens to be the same with regard to any given word, this is only because of the community of language. Art has a quality known as style. Style is a one-man language. Therefore, if it is difficult to sense the meaning of a work of art, this is because we too often try to apply to the components of it the associations which we are accustomed to applying to every-day language. This is ludicrous since art has to do with life and though logic may tend to intrude it will never be able to do so to the extent of obliterating style.

LIFE IS NOT LOGICAL

If life were logical, there would be no need for art.

It is not possible, or even desirable, to learn the various one-man languages which exist. They are not meant to be learnt. No-one can begin to realise anything about art until he can be unself-conscious about it. Art is created through feeling and through feeling it is received. Art is a form of communication. If one is thinking about it one will never begin to see what it is. There is no cleverness in art. A work of art must make its meaning clear directly to the subconscious. There must be no preliminary censorship. A poem is not a series of sentences. It is an integrated whole. This is the difference between literature and language. The images

"Other Voices" is looking for writers and painters who have realised this. Who know that " writing down " to an audience is just as much an intellectualism as writing up to an audience. All great works of art are immediately comprehensible to anyone who doesn't make the mistake of trying to understand them. If there were a few artists who were willing to propagate their work with the same vigour as the Communist Party there would soon be no more of this nonsense about the theory of painting/writing/music/sculpture/ etc. It is merely because so few works of art where they can be seen. Why don't people buy space on the walls of the London Underground and stick their paintings up. Why don't they duplicate their poems and stick them through people's letter boxes. These are not expensive things to do, and yet if they were implemented fully and regularly they would lead to a return to civilisation, a characteristic which man has lost recently.

It would soon be possible to hear a lecturer in the I.C.A. say, " I know what I like ! "

Ad vanishes

THE CRUCIFIX

AFTER CELLINI

Isobel English

In what dark country did she find herself now? The gloom inside the church was so heavy as to be felt ; it hung in great folds about her as she knelt in front of the altar. The black stiffened bow on the woman's hat at her side confused and distressed her ; it suggested a Maltese Cross, a denigration of the truth. A man's voice from the back of the Church made light of the responses.

Caroline cast her mind back to let in the light, for it seemed that no light could come from without. The priest's movements were respectful but inaccurate. A little of the cold water trickled down her neck as the stain of original sin was conditionally erased.

(" When we get married," Sebastian had said, " it will be a day of lightness and rejoicing. We'll have the altar massed with narcissus, and great golden bursts of Palestrina from the organ.") But to think back to those times now was as painfully difficult as the excavation of a buried city that had been laid waste after terrible defeat . . .

" Sebastian is all I have got." The first time he had taken her to the flat, his mother had bounced these words lightly over the rim of a tea-cup. She had been twenty-one with all the heavy brooding of prolonged adolescence. Later with a boldness that she would have described as straightforward, she had remarked : " Your Mother seems dreadfully possessive." She had not then known of her own cannibalistic streak : the desire to kill, dissect and devour. The necessary prerogative of the hunting woman was as yet a mystery hidden beneath the surface of restricted decencies that lead from church to grave.

The passion for post mortem was still young in her. As a stumbling infant that can only measure its strength by the violence of its falls, so she staggered about in a territory where the older and more worldly might fear to tread.

They had gone forward together in partnership (a joint interest in the book shop); yet in a sense it was she who followed doggedly after his frail willowy figure, basked in the radiance of his self obsessive projects, dubbed herself lieutenant so that she might further partake in the activities of his mind. " I want to run my own theatre, write my own plays and act in them." Sebastian at 23 was as indefatigable and hopeful as only the inexperienced can be. A sinuous Catholicism —an attitude of mind that set him on bartering terms with his God — made up for what his sensibilities and temperament lacked : " I have made terms with those of the next world. I have said : ' If you do this, I will do that ; and in all cases there have been answers.' " Caroline, in her own lack of faith, marvelled ; " If I could only believe as he does, we might draw closer together, there would not be this gulf of uncertainty between us." She could not pray in the sense of invoking any particular spiritual aid, but she made strange outward movements of the soul ; like a fish she floundered over dry land towards the Holy Sea.

One day they had sat together in his room until late in the afternoon ; locked together

Many years later, Stefan recounted to me the brief speech Russell had made to his friends at the celebration of his ninetieth birthday: "In the prime of my youth I considered myself rather strong in mathematics. Then, as my faculties deteriorated, I gave myself over to philosophy. In my old age, I was good for nothing but literature, and today, entirely senile, I concern myself with politics."

Stefan published his own work, of course, but also the work of young writers and poets, all more or less talented, whose ideas corresponded with his own. It was a small house, almost an underground one. That's how I got to know him. When I launched *Other Voices*, I had read some of his books and been greatly impressed. I wrote to him and that was that—we became friends.

STEFAN THEMERSON

Tell me about Other Voices.

Today, I think it's a real feat to produce a whole magazine—collecting all the texts, doing the layout, typesetting, and so on. I had a Polish printer who was already working for Themerson, but I set all the headlines myself by hand. Turning out six large-format pages every week and distributing them on my own, leaving aside the print and paper costs, was really a great deal of work. And I had to distribute them to bookshops myself, then return to collect the pennies. Six weeks of this finished me off. I caught pneumonia. It was fantasy, really, but at least it existed.

How did you find the necessary money?

On one of my nocturnal binges in London I came across a rather enthusiastic chap who loved making wildly extravagant bets. He spent the best part of his time in bars and pubs. And he was loaded. My plan appealed to him, and he advanced me the necessary funds. According to his shrink, the magazine gave him an interest in life. It was at this time that I painted *The Change*, the canvas now in the Tate. I did plenty of others, too, in the little place where I lived in Neal Street. I was under contract to the Redfern Gallery, who would send round their chauffeur in a Bentley convertible every week to pick up my work—something which made a great impression on my neighbors

RALPH RUMNEY, *THE CHANGE*, 1957

RALPH RUMNEY IN THE 1960s
PHOTO: H. SHUNK

He collected the takings?

Yes, I went off with the chauffeur to collect my check and put it in the bank.

How old were you?

Twenty, twenty-two. The Redfern's director, Rex Nankivell, bought all my work and gave me a contract. He handled promotion: he gave me a high profile in a big group show entitled "Metavisual, Tachiste, Abstract" in 1957. There was a woman in the story, married to the painter Patrick Heron. She fancied herself an intellectual. She was asked to develop her ideas in the catalog. I can't remember anymore who came up with this word "metavisual."

The Coffee House, Northumberland Avenue, 1954/55. A beautiful young man with a concave profile makes his entrance. He has strikingly blond hair, with a lock that keeps falling across his forehead. He speaks an impeccable English, and I get the strong impression that he's escaped from a public school. He's incredibly erudite—and so I'm immediately suspicious. He tells me he's just about to publish a literary review or an art magazine. Another upper-class cretin or a poseur, I think to myself. Eighteen at the most, queer for sure. In those days the word "gay" hadn't been adopted by the homosexual community. He looked to me like the sort who loved nothing better than causing a stir, another one of those vague chancers who has found his vocation in the Coffee House, that trail-blazing dive which brought together bohemians, down-and-outs, and Soho refugees, today transformed into a vast brothel of junk. He can see that I'm busy writing poetry but continues talking, trying to ensure that everyone gets a good look at him. I wouldn't trust him as far as I could throw him. I tell him that publishing a magazine costs money. He replies that he has an appointment with a gentleman. I believe he is talking about Mr. Sisson. Then he takes his leave, and I am sure I'll never see him again. He'll probably get picked up by some queer or some versatile nancy-boy. There was something very ambivalent about the young Mr. Rumney. To my great surprise and great dismay, he's back within the hour, his fists full of fivers. I attempt to hide my astonishment and the fact that I'm skint, obsessed by money and more especially by the lack of money. I swiftly

return to concentrating on my poem. And Ralph, he's offering coffees liberally to all the bums and beggars now crowding around him. That was it. *Other Voices* was born. And he was soon out selling it, shouting his wares, accosting anyone and everyone on the Charing Cross Road. Without the slightest inhibition. But then our Felix Krull disappeared. A year (or two) passed, and he was now popping into and out of our lives with decreasing regularity. And each time he laughingly suffered a sort of metamorphosis: an enormous change in his fortunes. We heard around that he was shacked up in a Venetian palace. With Ralph, anything was possible. Nothing came as a surprise. Apparently, he is betrothed to Pegeen, the daughter of Peggy Guggenheim, one of the richest creatures on this planet. So what's new? Erica and I are scraping a living by selling books from a barrow at Cambridge Circus. One winter day stands out. A taxi pulls up, and Ralph, unusually flustered, jumps out and hurries towards us. "Can you loan me a fiver? Quick!" he begs. "What?" Money is such a rare commodity, and this amount is a week's survival for us. "I've got Peggy Guggenheim in the taxi, and I've got to pay the cabby." "But she's the richest woman in the world." "I know, but she never carries any cash with her." I moan and hand over our day's takings, our worldly wealth, the last of our cash. We are now skint, but we laugh. What else can you do? Ralph was operating again. A Mephistophelian creature. He fits no category. But his actions keep alive the creative ideal, in the fog of the gloomiest days of the Cold War, long before the Beatles and the Age of Hype were to be unleashed on an unsuspecting, dangerous world.
BERNARD KOPS

She didn't know what it meant. And "abstract"—everyone around us could take it to mean whatever they liked. I wasn't at all happy with the title, but no one had asked me. Heron wasn't only a very famous artist in England, he was also art critic for the *New Statesman*. He must certainly have been very vexed to find himself in an inferior position to me, given the way the paintings were hung. This group show turned out to be effectively a one-man show for me: Rex had given me the whole ground floor. I invited Peggy Guggenheim to the opening. When she saw *The Change* she made a big fuss about buying it. She wanted to purchase it from me directly so as to avoid paying the gallery commission. I refused—the gallery had been loyal to me, and I saw no reason to cheat them. Nonetheless, I've always mistrusted the gallery world.

Do you know who advised her to buy the painting?

No, I haven't the slightest idea. Perhaps she genuinely liked it. There was no reason. For some time I had been a member of the Institute of Contemporary Arts, which was more or less founded by the Surrealists. One of the founders—the one I knew—was Roland Penrose. He was a curious character, a former Surrealist. Maybe he was the one who advised her.

Hadn't he been Peggy Guggenheim's lover?

Yes, exactly. But I didn't know that at the time. Anyway, Penrose worked for the British Council, an organization which was supposed to promote British art, culture, even the English language abroad. He was an extremely important man politically, if you like, someone I liked a lot, no kind of idiot. Of course, he could sometimes play a rather questionable role. In my case, he gave an official stamp to a kind of artism in which he tried to include me. Thanks to some kind of gut instinct, I had enough good sense to pull back at the last minute.

One day Baj, for whom I'd organized an exhibition in London, arranged to meet me at the opening of a Francis Bacon show at the Hanover Gallery. It was of his series of détournements of paintings by Van Gogh. It was there that I met Pegeen, Peggy Guggenheim's daughter. I was hit by the most classic, unexpected form of love at first sight. I tried to persuade her to come for a drink with some other people in a Soho club. A rich collector, a friend of Bacon, had invited her to a party at his place in Regent's Park. When I saw them leave, I grabbed a taxi and told the driver to follow them. We pursued them across town—it was quite an adventure. When I got to his place, it was quite obvious that all the men there were trying to pick up Pegeen. I must have been the only one who didn't know she was Peggy Guggenheim's daughter. Since she looked fed up, I suggested to her rather abruptly that we get out of there. I took her by the hand, she came back to my place, and that's how it all started.

Some days later her mother, still in pursuit of my painting, returned to the fray. I told her I couldn't sell it to her as it now belonged to Pegeen. She snarled at her: "You're fucking your way up to quite a collection!" The next day I received a card from Lady Norton announcing that she was coming to my studio the next day with Peggy. I was so disgusted at the thought of seeing her that I told Pegeen we should get out and go to Paris.

Pegeen was married at this time?

Yes, but she was already separated from her husband, the painter Jean Hélion. Her three children

COVER OF THE CATALOG FOR THE "METAVISUAL, TACHISTE, ABSTRACT" EXHIBITION

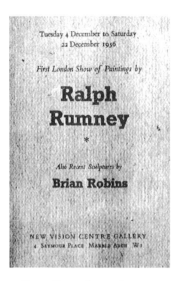

Tuesday 4 December to Saturday
22 December 1956

First London Show of Paintings by

Ralph
Rumney

*

Also Recent Sculptures by

Brian Robins

NEW VISION CENTRE GALLERY
4 SEYMOUR PLACE MARBLE ARCH W1

RALPH RUMNEY'S FIRST LONDON
EXHIBITION

were in Paris. We took a room in a hotel in Rue des Ciseaux. We hung out for a while in various places, particularly the Flore. Then we came back to London. I rented a flat that was more suitable than the place I was living before, in Covent Garden, which is now one of the most fashionable parts of London. But in those days we had gas lighting, and the toilets were out on the landing.

Gas light was perfect for painting. I was still very involved in the ICA and in all the polemics about art. At the ICA there was a group of individuals who had formed themselves into a sort of gang, a private club, something that was obviously quite sectarian. They called themselves the Independent Group. There were about a dozen of them: architects, theorists, art critics—no painters, as far as I know. I was invited once to give a seminar or a conference on the way in which the architects—the Design architects who were the nucleus of the Independent Group— had to some extent collaborated in the destruction of London.

Although excluded from that group, I had acquired some degree of power at the ICA. It was very small, but it allowed me to propose exhibitions. Not all my suggestions were accepted, but I was able to get exhibitions of Wols, Baj, Michaux, Klein, and Fontana, among others. The last two gave talks at the ICA.

It was Pegeen who told me about Wols. She'd put him up for a while not long before he died. No one knew him in London. With some effort, I managed to put together enough of his works on paper to make an exhibition.

Later, I organized lectures on the Situationists and the first screening of Guy Debord's *Hurlements en Faveur de Sade*—or *Howls for Sade*. Thanks to the title, there were crowds of people overflowing on to the stairway. When the lights went up after the

THE CONSUL | 30

first show, the audience protested so loudly that their shouts could be heard by those waiting outside. They tried to convince them to go home, but the atmosphere was so electric that their arguments had the opposite effect. The cinema was full to capacity for the second showing.

Did you stay long in London?

No, we quickly returned to Paris. All Pegeen's friends were there. I was beginning to earn quite a bit of money, and I received a small inheritance, which allowed me to buy a flat in Rue du Dragon: seventy-five square meters for three million old francs. I renovated the place from top to bottom so that Pegeen's three children could live with us. Their bedroom was scarcely larger than a cupboard; they slept in bunks, one above the other. We were living on top of each other, which didn't make it easy to paint. I would go to the Flore every day to try and read, to get away from the kids and all the distractions of family life. We were both painters. I needed to escape, to have some time to myself, even if it meant going to noisy cafés. It was around this time that I met Georges Bataille. He frequented the Flore, and I'd see him now and then. A seat would always be reserved for me by Pascal, an angel of a waiter. I'd take a book to the café every day. At this time, I was buying more or less everything published by Jean-Jacques Pauvert, especially Bataille's books. I was in the middle of reading one when Bataille asked Pascal: "Who is that young man reading my books whom you treat with such respect?" Actually, Pascal treated everyone with respect.

Si vous voulez être tenu
au courant de l'activité des
Éditions Jean-Jacques Pauvert
et recevoir gracieusement
NOTRE CATALOGUE ILLUSTRÉ, veuillez
nous retourner la présente carte
avec votre adresse complète.

M

Imprimé en Hollande

REPLY COUPON FROM EDITIONS
JEAN-JACQUES PAUVERT

And Bataille said he was a bit fed up with you?

Yes, because I was too young; it didn't seem righ
With Sartre or Bataille, that's how it always was.

Pascal said to him: "If you like, I can introduc
him to you." I heard this, got up and said: "I wi
introduce myself." And that led to a sort of frienc
ship between us. That was the way it was in Par
at the time. We would often meet each other in th
café. Bataille wrote a lot about eroticism, and whe
I didn't agree with his interpretations, I coul
discuss it with him. He was a polite man, a littl
shy, I think. I have a good memory of him, even
I can't remember our conversations, if you can se
the paradox.

Later, I got to know his friend Pierre Klossowsk
the brother of Balthus, whose paintings I admirec
He devoted a lot of his work to his wife. When h
wanted to adapt his novel *Roberte ce Soir* for a film
he proposed that I play the role of Jesus Christ an

fuck his wife. Absolutely not! We never spoke of it again, but I think he saw my limits.

The rest of the time I spent with Pegeen and the children. This rather idyllic life continued until Pegeen decided to go to Venice to see her mother. I don't know whether I should put it down to naïveté or stupidity, but I thought that some sort of reconciliation between mother and daughter was necessary for Pegeen's equilibrium. We rented a large flat in Castello, next to the police station. Pegeen refused to meet her mother unless I was present.

Through all this I got to meet a number of people whom I would never have known without her, including Malraux, John Cage, Stravinsky, and Jean Cocteau. When Pegeen was pregnant, Cocteau proposed himself as godfather for our son. He wanted me to make some stained-glass windows for a church, since he knew of my work on glass. Despite all the bad things Peggy said about me, Cocteau always stood by me.

Peggy Guggenheim was against you because of this business with the painting?

Not only that. She hated everything about me. I was always saying the wrong thing, always dropping clangers. For example, the first time I visited her she told me to take a glass and help myself to a whisky. There was a bottle of a rather prestigious single malt, so I poured myself a shot and tasted it. I have a relatively fine palate, and I realized that this was Japanese whisky that had been poured into another bottle. Innocently, I asked: "Peggy, where did you buy that? It's fake. You've been robbed." Pegeen begged me to shut up because it was Peggy herself who'd substituted the cheap whisky. I kept putting my foot in it like this.

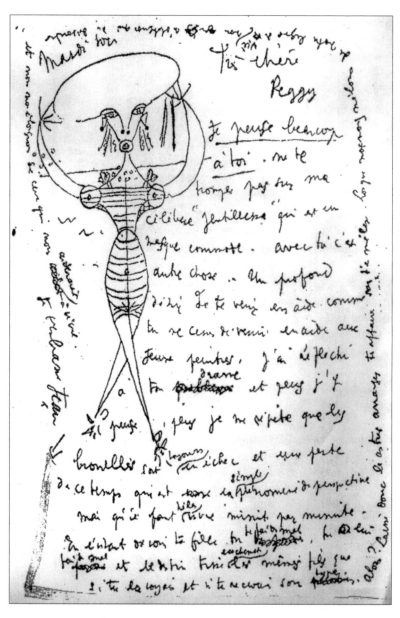

LETTER FROM COCTEAU TO PEGGY GUGGENHEIM

Through my mother-in-law, I acquired a terrible reputation, but, strangely enough, the people I met at her place would come to us to see my work. I had my own circle of true friends, like Alan Ansen, whom you'll find in the *Psychogeographic Guide to Venice;* a poet and writer, rather like Auden, a key figure in the Venetian scene at the end of the fifties and start of the sixties. He had a lifestyle that I would call hyper-Beat. He was very close to William Burroughs, Gregory Corso, and Allen Ginsberg. They were all arriving from Tangiers at this point, and since Alan had only a tiny flat, one or the other of them would sometimes stay with us. We all got on; everyone smoked hash. They quickly made themselves at home and emptied all my bottles. One day, Alan Ansen organized a poetry reading, well lubricated with alcohol and hashish. He had invited Peggy. In his opinion, the evening would offer a good opportunity for a reconciliation between the two of us. When she arrived she was given the best armchair. We would have put her on a throne if we'd had one. Allen Ginsberg began to read "Howl" and other texts. During the reading he became more and more impassioned and was soaked in sweat, exhausted. It was hot, and people were getting increasingly drunk. Allen pulled off his T-shirt and chucked it across the room. Disaster! It landed on Peggy's head. She made a scene and stormed out, saying that Stravinsky would never have behaved like that.

REVOLUTIONS ARE NOT SO MUCH ACCIDENTS OF ARMS AS ACCIDENTS OF LAWS.
SAINT-JUST

PINOT-GALLIZIO, PIERO SIMONDO, ELENA VERRONE, MICHÈLE BERNSTEIN, GUY DEBORD, ASGER JORN, AND WALTER OLMO IN COSIO D'ARROSCIA, JULY 1957
PHOTO: RALPH RUMNEY

WALTER OLMO
PHOTO: RALPH RUMNEY

What impression did Burroughs make on you?

I liked Burroughs, but he lived in a different world from me. But he was a great man. Our attitudes were very different. That story when he killed his wife, for example, that's not my style.

Let's go back to Paris. After you met Pegeen, did you stay in touch with the Letterists?

Nova dicere novo modo.
SAVONAROLA

I kept in contact with Debord, Wolman, and some of the others. I was invited to Cosio d'Arroscia. We went because one of Asger Jorn's friends, Piero Simondo, had an aunt who owned a hotel there. We stayed drunk for a week. Thus the Situationist International was born.

You're not in the family photo.

That's because I took it. I was the only person with a camera. Pegeen came with me but didn't participate. She thought it was my own private obsession.

There were Guy Debord, Michèle Bernstein, Walter Olmo, Elena Verrone, Piero Simondo, Gallizio, and Asger Jorn. And within this group there was a smaller one who were having their own conference within the conference: Debord, Michèle Bernstein, Jorn, and me. I do not remember any interventions from Olmo or Elena. Gallizio explained his production of industrial painting. And Piero seemed worried about the idea of the supersession of art. This doesn't mean that there were any intrigues or secret cabals. It's just that I don't recall them taking part in many of the theoretical debates.

To make our movement sound international I suggested that we should mention the London Psychogeographical Committee.

What was that?

Nothing at all. It was just me. I said: "OK, I'm the London Psychogeographical Committee." It was a pure invention, a mirage.

Psychogeography is one of the ideas with which I immediately felt total sympathy. Of course, it wasn't a new discovery, it had always existed. To cite just two examples, one can visit a counterfeit Lascaux and Bomarzo in northern Italy. The Letterists gave it a name and a methodology.

RALPH RUMNEY IN COSIO D'ARROSCIA
PHOTO: PEGEEN VAIL

What was decided in Cosio? What did you invent?

At the level of ideas, I don't think we came up with anything which didn't already exist. Collectively, we created a synthesis using Rimbaud, Lautréamont, and some others like Feuerbach, Hegel, Marx, the Futurists, Dada, the Surrealists, and the Vandals that Jorn was so fond of. We knew how to put all that together.

It is this putting into perspective that is original. When a movement is born, it starts from the point where the movement that preceded it stopped or failed. A series of influences across the centuries led to the Surrealist movement, and when the movement that was first Letterist then Situationist appeared, it was at precisely the point where its predecessor had come unstuck. In order to exist, it is necessary to synthesize all that was there before and say new things with new words.

GUY DEBORD, *REPORT ON THE CONSTRUCTION OF SITUATIONS*

Of the movements of the twentieth century, it is the Futurists, the Surrealists, the Letterists, Fluxus, and the Situationists which interest me. No doubt, there are a few missing, but those are the ones that come to mind right now.

For me, Dada could practically be reduced to Picabia, Duchamp, and a few others. It seems to me that Dada posed real questions in declaring that the work of art is only defined by the artist. The Futurists were really iconoclasts. That was what spurred their attacks on art and received ideas. Like Alcibiades, the first art critic, mutilating the genitals on the Hermae. Was he the first known iconoclast?

Apart from Duchamp himself, all these movements went through very rapid declines. For example, the Futurists turned to fascism, like wine turns to vinegar. The first restaurant where you ate art—long before Spoërri—was in Milan, run by Marinetti. There you ate hamburgers stuffed with lead, with lead shot. Quite a few people must have broken their teeth.

As for the Surrealists, well, they had their own sexual and political problems. And their biggest problem was André Breton, who was their Debord, if you like, or their Isou, or the two at once. He was a great man, no doubt, but one who little by little acquired delusions of grandeur and all that goes with it—expulsions, party lines. . . .

In the case of the Letterists, there are still some pale survivors of the time, but the important characters like Wolman and Dufrêne are dead. There are all kinds of post-Letterists, just as there are post-Surrealists and post-situs. Actually, they are cult followers. Which is a pity.

What was Jorn's attitude to the conference at Cosio?

He had a talent for organization. He loved everything to do with movements and conferences. Don't
forget that he'd been in the Resistance in Denmark:
he must have had to set up groups and networks at
the time. He was about twenty years older than us,
but he let us speak. He observed. He is one of the
few members of the Situationist International never
to have been expelled. He knew enough to resign
before that happened. He was the artist who stayed
the longest, while continuing to do whatever he
liked and see whomever he liked. You could say that
if there was an internal discipline within the SI that
prohibited any contact with expelled members, Jorn
cheerfully ignored it.

GIUSEPPE PINOT-GALLIZIO

Had you known of Debord's Report on the
Construction of Situations *before going to Cosio?*

I don't recall any session where this text could have
been voted on with any unanimity, since Olmo was
listening to Vivaldi, and I've no idea what some of
the others were thinking about or if they had understood it. The provincialism of the Italians at this
time was something I'd been struggling against for
two or three years. They believed people were con-
spiring against them, when in fact we were trying to
open their eyes.

*Debord first presented the text in its printed version
with a red cover . . .*

. . . saying that it was a subject for discussion and
that our discussions needed to be structured. We
had the plan to produce the *Internationale
Situationniste* journal. I proposed that we take ideas
for the inside layout from the *Cahiers* of the Collège

de Pataphysique and use metallic paper for the cover.

You had already used metal in your painting?

Yes, especially gold. If you look closely at *The Change*, you'll see some traces. I even taught Yves Klein my method of laying down gold leaf. I know that doesn't correspond to the official history, but that's what happened. Soon after Cosio, he came to my place in Venice. He had never seen gold leaf. Gold leaves are so thin that you can see light through them: they are transparent or "translucent," as I used to say at the time. I told him that you could also eat them and shoved one in his mouth. There is very little gold in these leaves. They're so fragile that you'll break them if you don't know how to handle them.

I learned how to work with them by reading texts from the fifteenth and sixteenth centuries, for gilders kept the methods secret. And I found them in Halifax, in the town's only artist supplier. I found out that you can get a whole multitude of tones from a gold leaf. The nuances are slight, but enchanting. And then there are all the colors they reflect. . . . Alice through the looking glass. Naturally, at first I only got fake gold, copper, etc., but I eventually found real gold leaf. There are several different kinds and a specific way of using each one. But I consider it to be a true color, just like aluminum or silver.

At what other time did you meet Yves Klein?

That brings us to an exhibition that took place in the Taptoë Gallery in Belgium in 1957. Asger Jorn had found this gallery, and we were supposed to prepare a Situationist exhibition. This was just before the foundation of the SI. Guy Debord, Michèle Bernstein, Asger Jorn, Pierre Simondo, and I were all supposed to exhibit something, as was Yves Klein, even though he wasn't a Situationist and Debord couldn't stand the sight of him. He couldn't bear him because in his view he was not ideologically sound and couldn't be converted. Nonetheless, Debord had one of his paintings, which Klein had given him. This exhibition gave rise to an incident which says much about Guy Debord's excessive character. Asger had received a telegram from Debord—he was a specialist in telegrams—saying that he wasn't going to come. Asger and I took a helicopter to go and get him in Paris. When we were leaving to go back to Brussels on the train, Guy and I had arranged to meet Jorn on the platform at the Gare du Nord.

Jorn wasn't on the platform, but had already got into a carriage. We waited for him until departure time. I advanced the hypothesis that he might already be on the train. Guy refused to go and look because he was convinced that we were supposed to meet on the platform and nowhere else. I took the train. Jorn and I tried to get Guy to come later, but he was furious. He elevated this little event to such heights of evil that it became a work of art. He didn't come to the Taptoë Gallery, and none of his work was exhibited. But that was Guy's genius. He had a gift for détournement.

MAN IS ONLY DEPENDENT WHEN HE HAS BEGUN TO CIVILIZE HIMSELF WITHOUT PRINCIPLES.
SAINT-JUST

GUY DEBORD IN COSIO
PHOTO: RALPH RUMNEY

Of things or of people?

Both. He tried to do it with me . . . and it is true that I was greatly influenced by him.

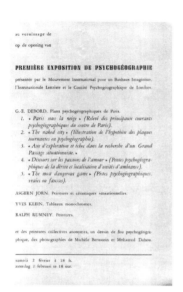

PROGRAM FOR THE EXHIBITION AT THE
TAPTOË GALLERY

In the exhibition catalog it says that it was held in the Taptoë Gallery from the 2nd to the 26th of February and was entitled "First Exhibition of Psychogeography."

Yes, that's possible.

It was organized by the International Movement for an Imaginist Bauhaus, the Letterist International, and the London Psychogeographical Committee. There were five works by Debord, which were psychogeographical maps of Paris . . .

. . . which never arrived.

There were paintings and ceramics by Asger Jorn, monochrome paintings by Yves Klein, paintings by Ralph Rumney, anonymous collective paintings, a drawing by a mad psychogeographer, and photographs by Michèle Bernstein and Mohammed Dahou.

Michèle and Mohammed didn't participate.

And this drawing by a mad psychogeographer?

I don't know. To be honest, this was a period of considerable confusion and drunkenness. The uncertainty came from Debord's lack of clarity about his decision not to come. We kept phoning him, without success. The result of the exhibition was that, despite everything, in the end Asger was poorer than me. I don't know why: he had to pay for a lot of things. I took him to London to see Guy Atkins.

You got him to sell a painting?

Yes.

Before we leave the Taptoë, there was an announcement of a talk by Ralph Rumney on the 4th of February, "The Art Brut of Living." Does this mean anything to you?

That was my perennial theme. It coincides with a little saying of Dufrêne's: "To be an artist is to live as an artist." Which does not mean to adopt all the usual clichés. When I was in Milan, for example, I wore a dark raincoat, a bowler hat (my fascination for bowler hats comes from Delvaux's paintings), and a carefully rolled umbrella. Dressing like this seemed to me more intelligent than going around in rags with long hair. Moreover, it shocked the Milanese, who didn't think that artists were supposed to walk around like that.

There were other talks, too. There was one by Jorn entitled "Industry and Fine Art: The Two Extremes of Situationist Unity." A typically Jornian title, that. And the following day there was a monosonorous talk by Yves Klein.

Which was extremely boring.

What was it like?

It anticipated Warhol and his film on the Empire State Building, which lasted twenty-four hours. Klein's talk consisted of a recorded sound which lasted a long time. Intellectually, it was a very interesting concept, and it should have stayed like that. But Yves liked to actualize his concepts.

Dalí, for instance, had the notion of displaying a huge baguette right across the Place de la Concorde. He didn't see the point in actually doing it. I don't know if Klein knew of Dalí's idea, but he must have been aware of it by osmosis. The sonorous talk was less important and a lot more annoying than Dalí's texts. There is a real difference between an idea and its realization. There lies the whole paradox of conceptual art. I tend to think that Dalí's writings were more important than his paintings, even though he achieved many things. As he said himself, he was a paranoiac madman. He invented something. He believed that his strength lay in that, and indeed it did. His achievements were beneath his ideas, whereas I would say the contrary of Klein. You see, people often have the failing of having ideas which go beyond what is possible. Not necessarily physically impossible, because one can always get round technical impossibilities. But it is much rarer to be able to circumvent political impossibilities. And that is why art is dangerous. Both Dalí and Klein were individuals who veered towards the extreme right. But I am not willing to attack Klein, whom I have always considered to be one of my best friends.

What memories do you have of the Taptoë event?

One evening when we were drunk, Jorn, Klein, and I made a painting, but I cannot remember a thing about making it. I've seen a color reproduction of it, with our three signatures. After all, that's the proof that we did it together. I can recognize the part that I made and the part made by Jorn. Apart from a bit of blue, I can't see where Klein came in. And it's not Klein blue, at least not in the reproduction. But he signed it, so he must have participated. The advocate of collective paintings was Jorn. All I can presume is that when we were in Brussels, waiting for Debord, Michèle, and the others, waiting for Godot, and being a bit drunk or having nothing better to do, we painted this picture. But I would not be able to tell you where or who bought the colors.

ASGER JORN, YVES KLEIN, RALPH RUMNEY,
UNTITLED, 1957

You must have all been together later, with the others?

Yes. We had to make this first real Situationist exhibition. The true reason for Guy's absence was perhaps that he was able to predict that it would be a failure. I remember the opening, the gallery, the lavish dinners at the Canterbury restaurant hosted by Niels, who had bought a big painting by Jorn, *Letter to My Son*, today in the Tate. He would invite people he wanted to see into a private room. One evening, we were in this room and oysters were brought in. They were large, flat oysters, a bit like the ones you get in England from Whitstable or Colchester. There was a flunkey who opened them, and Niels made a passionate speech about the correct way to eat an oyster. You see, you put it in your mouth like this and then you bite, and remember that it is alive. You kill it.

On the evening of the opening, we got pissed with some students from the University of Brussels and made a psychogeographical tour of the city, which was then being rebuilt in full Buchanization. We stopped in all the bars we found on the way, and they led us to the Manneken-Pis. I didn't know that they had such unusual things down there nor that it was the pride of Brussels. The consequence of all the wandering from bar to bar was that I pissed on the Manneken-Pis, which was rather well received by the students and passersby.

You had not abandoned your own research into psychogeography?

Especially not in Venice. I was quite fascinated by the *fotoromanzi*, those magazines of photo stories mainly aimed at female readers. I decided to use one for my own purposes and to create a kind of psychogeographic map of Venice. The town lent itself perfectly to such an exercise because of its labyrinthine nature. And the thing that struck me most was that when people go to San Marco, they are encouraged to look at the mosaics above their heads. In my case, maybe because I have a slightly hunched back or for whatever reason, I looked at the ground. Those geometric figures are extremely complex and extremely detailed, with square forms. I don't know how to explain it, but squares—Polaroids, for example—have always fascinated me. A lot of my paintings are square. I still dream of making square films.

To square Wolman's circle?

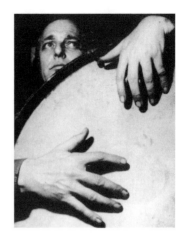

ASGER JORN

In Cosio, I had already proposed making a psycho-geographic exploration of Venice. In reality, this détournement wasn't called the *Psychogeographic Guide to Venice* but *The Leaning Tower of Venice.* The plan was to create a sketch which would show the areas where no one went, far from the Grand Canal. The idea was to de-spectacularize Venice by suggesting unknown routes through it. Psychogeography is concerned with places and the emotional states they provoke. Venice, like Amsterdam and the Paris of yesteryear, offers many possibilities for disorientation.

It was for this reason that Debord and Jorn undertook explorations in Paris and Denmark, to unearth the secrets of those urban depths. In Cosio, I proposed different things: first, that I make a psycho-geographic exploration of Venice. The title came from the fact that in the first photo there is the leaning tower, like the Leaning Tower of Pisa. It seems that they have just hired someone from China to put it straight.

They don't know what to do to straighten it. And no one seriously imagines they can do it. It is rather that they are trying to keep it from falling down.

I knew how to straighten it. You know, sometimes one can find answers that others can't see. If the tower topples over, too bad. I made a second proposal to the SI. I had read that there were certain products you could put in water. If you pour them into a spring, they will color the water and you can discover the underground route of the waters.

Around 1957, they discovered the source of Petrarch's fountain in Ile-sur-la-Sorgue by introducing a colorant into the rivers and springs upstream. I had read that in a newspaper and said to myself that with a bit of money one could pour colorants into the Venetian canals at specific points in order to observe the circulation of waters within the city. That was more or less my plan. Five years later, some Argentinian artist, whose name escapes me, threw some green substance into the canal from the Accademia bridge as a stunt.

I never carried out my plan. His wasn't important—it was merely a matter of trying to shock people, and, since he couldn't get any color but green and the waters of Venice are already green, it had no effect. I wanted to put in red, you see, in order to observe and study the currents and people's reactions.

To come back to The Leaning Tower of Venice—*it took the form of a photo story?*

Yes, and moreover you cannot fail to notice that the SI made a lot of détournements of photo novels. I suggested all that. What is called *The Guide* isn't a guide at all.

It was announced in Potlatch *No. 29 in November 1957 with the title* Psychogeographical Venice.

In Cosio, I think I talked a lot about photo novels and the possibilities for the SI's publishing détourned photos.

Anthropometric photos?

Yes.

That was your idea?

Yes, and Guy's irony was to use it in the first issue of the journal to make public my expulsion, because my proposal in Cosio, which was adopted and quickly forgotten, was that each member of the SI should present themselves in the first issue with a little note preceded by an anthropometric photo, a mug shot.

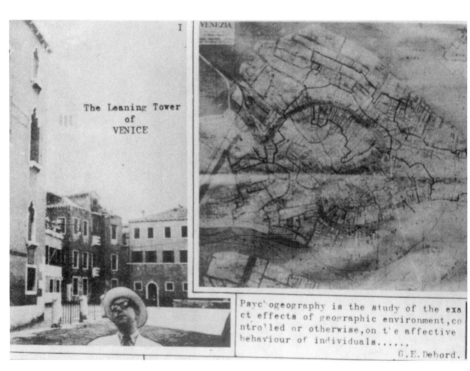

The first pictures in *The Leaning Tower of Venice*

With your taste for photo stories, how did you come to turn them round, to tell a different story, to develop a theory?

At the time I wanted to make films. But I only had a Rolleiflex, so I could only make a photo story. The photo story, you know, it's a pretty girl and a handsome boy, like a popular romance. I put mine together with whatever came to hand. I see Ansen in front of a bit of graffiti, something rare at the time, and you can see that it says "Hollywood." The second photo offers a route through Venice. It's very hard to see it clearly, because I had difficulty in photographing the documents. But there's a trace there, and even if it's not exactly the same, it also exists on the map of Venice. Debord and Jorn also reinvented towns by playing with maps and plans.

The Guide *was the pretext for your expulsion, wasn't it?*

Yes. I did eventually complete it, but a little later than Guy's planning permitted. He claims that was what led to my expulsion, even though, as Michèle Bernstein says, Guy did not always reveal the true reasons for expulsions.

In *Potlatch*, the *Guide*'s publication was already announced. In the first issue of *Internationale Situationniste* you read that I have been expelled because of being late.

I don't know what reasons they had, Michèle and Guy. My life was extremely complicated at the time. Pegeen was pregnant with my son, Sandro. Jean Hélion, the painter, her first husband, had sent a notary from Paris denying his paternity of the baby, although he behaved very well towards Sandro later. I suppose it was his lawyers who pushed him to do it. Their divorce still hadn't gone through. I was English, Pegeen American. I consulted international lawyers: the child should be born in Switzerland.

PSYCHOGEOGRAPHY. Study of the precise effects of the geographical milieu, whether consciously arranged or not, and its direct influences on the affective behavior of individuals. PSYCHOGEOGRAPHER. One who studies and communicates psychogeographical realities. *INTERNATIONALE SITUATIONNISTE*, No. 1

It's the best place for an illegitimate child. On the eve of our departure we had a farewell dinner with some friends. Pegeen started getting contractions right in the middle of it. Fortunately enough, one of those present was our gynecologist! We got Pegeen into hospital. It was a complicated delivery. In the end, our son was born.

What was his nationality?

He was stateless. Hoping to please Peggy, the British consul in Venice refused to register the birth. He couldn't be Italian because in that country there is no right to citizenship through birth. I phoned my mother-in-law's lawyer, a man named Trupiano. He advised me to have a photograph taken of the baby in my arms. He stuck the photo on a declaration he had drawn up on *carta bollata* by which I recognized the child as mine. We went to the office of the vice prefect; Trupiano suggested the vice prefect go and make himself a coffee, and while he was away he stamped the document to make it valid.

I deeply regret having lost this piece of paper. I could have made it into a collage. I went to Switzerland with my son. When we got to the British consulate, the baby was registered on my passport. It was an amazing document; they had written: "Sandro Rumney, son of Ralph Rumney. Born of an unknown mother."

So for your own son you arranged something quite Dadaist!

Not arranged, endured. A little later, Pegeen and I went back to London and were able to get married. My son at last managed to get his own passport— poor little bastard!

And you gave him an Italian first name?

Sandro, as in Botticelli. Actually, there's more to it than romanticism. If you live in several countries, you need a name that can be pronounced in the three or four languages you speak.

A detail which shows you are methodical in all things.

If you like. Sandro can be pronounced just as well in French as in Italian, Greek, or even Spanish.

Your expulsion was announced in the first issue of Internationale Situationniste *in a short text headed "Venice Has Conquered Ralph Rumney."*

RALPH RUMNEY'S PASSPORT

I tried to send my work in time for it to appear in the journal, but the original document only reached Impasse de Clairvaux where Debord lived two months after it came out. Michèle and Guy considered that the birth of a child was a bit of foolishness that should not distract a true revolutionary from his path.

It seems to me that if your wife is pregnant, it is your duty to be involved. I was overtaken by events, which would be a kind of translation of what you find in the text about my expulsion. I even merited a compliment which I find somewhat exaggerated. It is true that I "succeeded in establishing the basic elements of a map of Venice in which the notational technique plainly surpasses all previous psychogeographic cartography." But we should not forget Ivan Chtcheglov, who was the real inventor of psychogeography.

VENICE HAS CONQUERED RALPH RUMNEY

In the spring of 1957, the British Situationist Ralph Rumney had embarked on a number of psychogeographic surveys of Venice, and had subsequently set himself the goal of exploring the city systematically, hoping to be able to present a complete report on his findings by about June 1958. . . . At first, the enterprise progressed well. . . . But by the month of January 1958, bad news began to reach us. Beset by countless difficulties and increasingly sucked into the milieu he had tried to traverse, Rumney had to abandon one line of inquiry after another, until finally, as he communicated to us in his moving message of 20 March, he found himself reduced to a position of total inertia. Heavy were the losses among those explorers of old to whom we owe our understanding of objective geography. We must expect casualties, too, among the new seekers of knowledge, the explorers of social space. . . . The pitfalls are of a different kind, just as what is at stake is of a different nature: the aim, now, is to make life a passionate adventure. And this, of course, brings us up against all the defenses of a world of boredom. Rumney has disappeared, and his father has yet to start looking for him. Thus it is that the Venetian jungle has shown itself to be the stronger, closing over a young man, full of life and promise, who is now lost to us, a mere memory among so many others.

INTERNATIONALE SITUATIONNISTE, No. 1

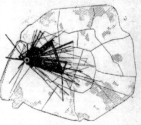

INTERNATIONALE SITUATIONNISTE

● **VENISE A VAINCU RALPH RUMNEY**

Le situationniste britannique Ralph Rumney qui avait mené dès le printemps de 1957 quelques reconnaissances psychogéographiques dans Venise, s'était ultérieurement fixé pour but l'exploration systématique de cette agglomération, et espérait pouvoir en présenter un compte rendu exhaustif autour de juin 1958 (cf. une annonce du n° 29 de *Potlatch*). L'en reprise se développa d'abord favorablement. Rumney, qui était parvenu à établir les premiers éléments d'un plan de Venise dont la technique de notation surpassait nettement toute la cartographie psychogéographique antérieure, faisait part à ses camarades de ses découvertes, de ses premières conclusions, de ses espoirs. Vers le mois de janvier 1958, les nouvelles devinrent mauvaises. Rumney, aux prises avec des difficultés sans nombre, de plus en plus attaché par le milieu qu'il avait essayé de traverser, devait abandonner l'une après l'autre ses lignes de recherches et, pour finir, comme il nous le communiquait par son émouvant message du 20 mars, se voyait ramené à une position purement statique.

Les anciens explorateurs ont connu un pourcentage élevé de pertes au prix duquel on est parvenu à la connaissance d'une géographie objective. Il fallait s'attendre à voir des victimes parmi les nouveaux chercheurs, explorateurs de l'espace social et de ses modes d'emploi.

Les embûches sont d'un autre genre, comme l'enjeu est d'une autre nature : il s'agit de parvenir à un usage passionnant de la vie. On se heurte naturellement à toutes les défenses d'un monde de l'ennui. Rumney vient donc de disparaître, et son père n'est pas encore parti à sa recherche. Voilà que la jungle vénitienne a été la plus forte, et qu'elle se referme sur un jeune homme, plein de vie et de promesses, qui se perd, qui se dissout parmi nos multiples souvenirs.

Relevé de tous les trajets effectués en un an par une étudiante habitant le XVIe Arrondissement. Publié par Chombart de Lauwe dans « Paris et l'agglomération parisienne ». (P.U.F.)

Ralph Rumney

Did you know him?

No, he was already confined to an institution by the time I came to Paris.

Have you anything to say about your expulsion?

Yes, I would make two points. I was expelled politely, even amiably. And the expulsion displayed Guy's sense of irony. All the more so because I recall having said in Cosio that any lack of the fanaticism necessary for our advancement must be punished by expulsion.

If your expulsion was handled rather charmingly, the same cannot be said of that of the Italians: "The conference proceeded to a purge of the Italian section where a fraction had given its support to theses that were idealist and reactionary. This fraction refused to make any self-criticism after their theses were refuted and condemned by the majority. The conference therefore decided to expel Walter Olmo, Piero Simondo, and Elene Verrone." Not one word more.

Indulgence, in all its forms, remains the primary moral deficiency.
GUY DEBORD

Yes, that was harsh.

How did you react when you heard of your expulsion?

It hit me very hard. It was very demoralizing. I really believed in the SI, and I still do. You don't have to become a turncoat because you've been excommunicated. I would claim that at the Cosio conference I made a real contribution to the foundation of the SI.

Were you expelled only because of the delay in delivering the Psychogeographic Guide to Venice?

As I've already said, Debord didn't always give the real reasons for expulsions. And indeed he didn't really need to. The motives for expulsions published in *Potlatch* and *Internationale Situationniste* bore no relation to the real reasons. There were two contradictory criteria for expulsion. On the one hand, incompetence and inefficiency, often tolerated until they became glaring—a matter of the SI's proclaimed equality, which hid the fact that Guy knew he was more equal than the others—and on the other hand, a mind that was too brilliant: I need only mention Dufrêne and Wolman. There were always these two different reasons. There's an anecdote that is exemplary in this respect. One day,

François Dufrêne met Guy in the street. He offered his hand in greeting. Ignoring his hand, Guy proclaimed: "From today on, I will never speak to you again." He never said another word to him and never gave any explanation.

Was Dufrêne hurt?

Terribly. Guy told me of the incident with pride. François was mortally wounded. I learned this when I started meeting him in the Lara Vincy Gallery. I began to spend time with him and Gil Wolman. I quickly understood two things: the first was that he had been grievously hurt by this split, and the second was that he hadn't deserved it. He considered Guy Debord to be his best friend. I think it was being unable to understand why it happened that was the worst part.

Why was Wolman expelled?

As with the others, we didn't know the real reason. Unlike François, who never got over the separation, Gil rose above it. At least, that's the impression he gave. He was morbidly modest.

When you all met up again, there was this common denominator in the fact that all three of you had been expelled in successive periods.

Yes, but we didn't talk about it. In any case, I cannot imagine Gil and Guy together in the SI. The SI could not be bicephalous. We met up again at the beginning of the sixties after our respective expulsions that had more or less coincided. No longer being a member of the SI, I saw no reason not to see them. At the start of the seventies, Wolman and I lived in the same street. We saw each other a lot and exchanged ideas. Gil had a great sense of humor. He was brilliant. Michèle Bernstein, who did not follow the principle of expulsion, was a good friend of his. One could consider Gil as a painter in the oral tradition. He made a record with Jean-Louis Brau.

The Megapneumics.

Yes, Megapneumonia or something like that.

No, Megapneumics, not Megapneumonia!

Yes. And he produced *The Anticoncept*, he put his name to the "User's Guide to Détournement" (which is a fundamental text) with Debord, he developed *Scotch Art*, and he created true masterpieces like *Les Séparations*, *Les Inhumations*, which are astonishing examples of what he called unpainted painting. To earn a living, he invented *The Gallery Guide*. Every time I had an exhibition he would give me a page for free. It was very useful. He was a delightful man, you know. I was also a pal of Dufrêne. So we often saw each other. When I passed his door, I'd often just drop in. He was always available.

GIL J WOLMAN

On the off chance?

Yes, he was someone with whom you never needed an appointment. And if you wanted to see him, he'd come straight away. He had a bar in his flat. Knowing my habits, he would open a bottle for me.

Gil made a great impression on me when I met him. He was a very powerful character. He really opened up something new.

Absolutely, I miss him. There's not much I can add. He was an intellectual companion, a drinking

L'histoire du cinéma est pleine de morts d'une grande valeur marchande. Alors que le butin et l'intelligence découvrent une fois de plus le vieillard Chaplin et bêvent d'admiration au dernier remake surréaliste de Luis Buñuel, les lettristes qui sont jeunes et beaux poursuivent leurs ravages :

Les écrans sont des miroirs qui pétrifient les aventuriers, en leur renvoyant leurs propres images et en les arrêtant. Si ont ne peut pas traverser l'écran des photos pour aller vers quelque chose de plus profond, le cinéma ne m'intéresse pas

Jean-Isidore ISOU

Avril 1951 :

TRAITÉ DE BAVE ET D'ÉTERNITÉ

C'est fini le temps des poètes
Aujourd'hui je dors.
Février 1952 : ou J WOLMAN

L'ANTICONCEPT
(interdit par la censure)

« Les yeux fermés j'achète tout au printemps. »
Guy-Ernest DEBORD
Juin 1952 :

HURLEMENTS EN FAVEUR DE SADE

En cours de réalisation :

LA BARQUE DE LA VIE COURANTE
de Jean-Louis BRAU

DU LÉGER RIRE QU'IL Y A AUTOUR DE LA MORT
de Serge BERNA

NOUS FAISONS LA RÉVOLUTION
A NOS MOMENTS PERDUS

companion, a neighbor. I know few people like that. I miss him greatly.

And what about Wolman's work, his creations?

His film *The Anticoncept* was banned at the time. It's a magnificent film.

He says in it: "The time of poets is over. Today I'm sleeping." And the final sentence: "I am immortal and I am alive."

It's incomparable.

There is a section of sound poetry in it which is superb.

Yes, and I think Debord made his afterwards.

First there was Isidore Isou's film, Treatise on Spit and Eternity *in 1950, then* The Anticoncept *by Gil J Wolman in 1951, and finally Debord's* Howls for Sade *in 1952. Debord and Wolman had been cosignatories of texts in the Belgian Surrealist journal,* Les Lèvres Nues. *What was your position with regard to the Surrealists?*

I agreed with everyone else about how to deal with the last Surrealists and Dadaists who were still hanging around in the area.

It was an exquisite corpse that was beginning to give off a bad smell. When we saw Tristan Tzara coming out of the Deux Magots with his ridiculous hat on his head, we'd run after him and shove it down over his eyes. We called him a renegade, which wasn't entirely wrong. But I must say that molesting a little old man like that is one of the rare things in my life that I would rather not have done.

Burn and destroy in order to renew!

It was childish, but we wanted to make a point. One thing is sure—we were at war with Breton.

During the war, he went to New York. It was said that he worked for the CIA or the OSS, as it was then called.

What we know is that he made radio broadcasts denouncing the Nazis and the Pétainists, which is entirely to his credit. His defenders say that is all he did. Others claim that he played a part in the American takeover and domination of the European art market and of the development of art after the war. I know nothing about this. There are suspicions, that's all. Breton played a rather shady role after working with the Americans. I think that he continued to work with them after he returned to Paris, and art suffered the consequences.

BANNING ORDER FOR *THE ANTICONCEPT*

According to your argument, the American secret services played a role in French art, even in European art in general.

You're trespassing on a project I've been researching for the past two years! Frances Stoner Saunders's book *Who Paid the Piper?* published not long ago in London, reveals what Grémoin and others could only suspect.

Breton thought that he could not assert himself without the support of an international movement . . .

. . . in which he had the power to admit or expel.

And the Letterists were very critical of the Surrealist movement . . .

. . . while imitating it.

Tract announcing the conference,
"Surrealism: Dead or Alive?"

Did Debord behave like Breton?

Yes, exactly. A Jacobin—the great historical error of
the French Revolution, which gave birth to
Stalinism.

*If you look at the ritual of expulsions and other methods
used by the SI, they're comparable to the practices of religious sects—millenarian movements, for example.*

Yes, you could say that. Every contestatory movement, of whatever kind, will always, despite itself,
reproduce the structures of the organization it challenges. Thus, even if it "succeeds," it changes
more or less rapidly into an imitation of what it has
opposed.

*In Debord's books we can find allusions to mystical
and religious texts, quotes from Ecclesiastes, from
Bossuet. . . .*

Along with references to Jakob Boehme, who was
important for him. People like St. Bernard or
Abélard, who needed to control something they had
created, of which they were both the source and the
supervisor.

*Did you go to Guy Debord's lecture on 18 November
1957, "Surrealism: Dead or Alive?"*

No, but it had quite an influence on lots of interventions that I was later to make, not so much in the
substance as in the form. Guy had recorded his
speech on a tape recorder, which he switched on
and sat beside, a glass in his hand, without saying
anything.

I sort of plagiarized this speech at the Beaubourg for an exhibition of an arsehole called Michel Bulteau. After half an hour, he decided it was too boring and switched off the tape recorder. Gil Wolman was in the audience, and he got up and said, "If there are only cunts here, me and Ralph are leaving." I walked off the platform, joined him on the stairs, and we headed off to a bistro.

Plagiarism is necessary. It is implied in the idea of progress. It clasps an author's sentence tight, uses his expressions, eliminates a false idea, replaces it with the right idea.
ISIDORE DUCASSE
(COMTE DE LAUTRÉAMONT)
(trans. Paul Knight,
Harmondsworth: Penguin, 1978)

Hadn't Debord already done something similar?

Yes, a bit earlier. It happened after the IVth Conference of the SI in London. Guy Atkins and Debord had asked me to translate the conference resolution into English. Shit, I worked through the night and produced what I think was quite a good translation. Atkins told me that there were some sentences in the French which needed to be adapted so they would be clear in English.

Obviously.

They had to be changed. I turned up an hour before the start of the conference, bearing the translation. Debord and Jacqueline de Jong scrutinized it at great length and told me that it wasn't word for word, it wasn't accurate. I had to redo it. So I go to the office across the road and redo it, word for word. The conference has to be held up for two hours. I'm knocking it out very quickly, because it's starting to get on my nerves.

I bring them the text. They had asked the public to wait because of a problem with translation or a technical problem or whatever. The room was full, and the best thing they could come up with was to give the text to Maurice Wyckaert to read aloud.

MICHÈLE BERNSTEIN

The Fleming?

His pronunciation rendered it completely incomprehensible. And they had made him read the literal, word-for-word version—which was incomprehensible in the first place, even before being read in Flemish. Guy Atkins, Debord, Jacqueline de Jong, I, and a few others all sat in one row and loudly applauded every sentence. Then a young Englishman got up and said he wanted to ask a question. Toni del Renzio, who was chairing the session, let him speak. "What," he asked, "is Situationism?" Debord, who was no doubt looking for a pretext, said "If there are only cunts here, we are leaving." The whole row got up, and we went off to the pub. I don't think one could have wished for a more spectacular event.

Did you know Michèle Bernstein at the same time as the other Letterists?

Yes, at the start of the fifties. She was unlike the other girls we knew, for several reasons. She was already Debord's girlfriend. She wasn't the type of girl that the men at Moineau's would pass around.

I think there was a deep understanding between Guy and Michèle; they seemed to see eye to eye about everything. I don't know what else you need to be a couple. Anyway, that was my impression. I thought they were wonderful.

After they separated, she managed to keep her independence from him. Even though Guy helped her find her way, she was never under his thumb. Indeed, I think I influenced him. And then, you know, in a milieu where most people didn't work and had no income, she had a job. I remember spending a night in Impasse de Clairvaux where they lived. There wasn't much space, but at least they had a place of their own. Their generosity was boundless, a kind of absolute potlatch. Sometimes they would take me out to eat. They got me to discover Paris or at least that limited part of it that goes from the Contrescarpe to Saint-Germain-des-Prés, via Rue de la Huchette.

And you made your living by selling paintings?

Not at all. I didn't work. I and the rest of the tribe were extremely disreputable, scruffy, scurrilous, and penniless. When we left Moineau's we seldom knew where we were going to sleep. It was more or less the only place where we were welcome or at least well received. Passing for existentialists, we were part of the local fauna. We occasionally managed to con tourists, offering them guided tours of Saint-Germain-des-Prés. More or less vagrants, we would beg in the streets from time to time to pay for drinks. Our social exclusion made us into a closed group.

The Moineau gang created for itself a kind of informal family, a tribe.

Yes, we formed a kind of gang. We passed around tips, like how to steal alcohol from the cellar of an illegal drinking den. I stole quite a few bottles. One night, one of the gang, perhaps it was Pierre Feuillette, started drinking and, instead of carrying off the bottles, drank them on the spot, got pissed out of his head, and fell asleep. That was the end of that one. We helped each other out. If someone managed to find a hotel room, he shared it. We'd get six or seven people in. Sometimes we'd find a room in Rue des Canettes. Full of lice but just about affordable. But having said all that, I should add that being one of the youngest, and English to boot, I wasn't completely accepted by the others.

The fourth session, on the 27th, adopted a resolution concerning the imprisonment of Alexander Trocchi and decided on the attitude to adopt to the Institute of Contemporary Arts, where Wyckaert is to make a public declaration on behalf of the Conference. Everyone agreed that this circle of modernist aesthetes should be treated with contempt.
INTERNATIONALE SITUATIONNISTE, No. 5

GUY DEBORD, *MORT DE J.H. OU FRAGILES TISSUS (EN SOUVENIR DE KAKI)*,
MÉTAGRAPHIE, MARCH, 1954

What would you say most distinguished the way you lived?

In my case, you could say that it was the dérive. I began to understand what it was through Debord, not so much because he talked about it, but because he practiced it. And ever since I have never, or hardly ever, done anything else. My whole life became a dérive. I was gripped, fascinated by the idea.

What did the dérive mean in Paris?

We wandered from café to café—we went where our feet and our inclinations carried us. We had to get by with very little. I still wonder how it was that we managed to survive. Our dérives in Paris took place in a very restricted space. We discovered routes to go from one place to another that were really detours. Later, we put this into practice in Amsterdam. In Cosio, I suggested the idea of simultaneous dérives where the different participants would keep in contact via walkie-talkies. But we didn't possess any. For me, Paris remained for a long time an area enclosed by Montparnasse, Saint-Germain-des-Prés, and Rue de la Huchette. For example, I didn't discover the Butte-aux-Cailles district until much later. The same goes for the rest of the thirteenth arrondissement, Rue Jeanne d'Arc, Rue du Château-des-Rentiers, which was not far from the studio I had later on.

René Crevel did his own détournement on Rue du Château-des-Rentiers—Rentiers' Castle Street—by rechristening it Rue du Taudis-des-Chômeurs—Slum of the Unemployed Street.

I would sometimes spend the night in the Salvation Army hostel down there. It was the district where

Certain streets in Paris are as degraded as a man covered with infamy; also, there are noble streets, streets simply respectable, young streets on the morality of which the public has not yet formed an opinion; also cut-throat streets, streets older than the age of the oldest dowagers, estimable streets, streets always clean, streets always dirty, working, labouring, and mercantile streets. In short, the streets of Paris have every human quality, and impress us, by what we must call their physiognomy, with certain ideas against which we are defenceless. There are, for instance, streets of a bad neighbourhood in which you could not be induced to live, and streets where you would willingly take up your abode.
HONORÉ DE BALZAC, FROM *FERRAGUS, CHIEF OF THE DEVORANTS* (trans. Katharine Prescott Wormeley, Project Gutenberg Etext, 1999)

Léo Malet spent his youth. In the days of the Letterists, you couldn't say there was any kind of official zone because there was no rule preventing anyone from leaving it. In practice, we confined ourselves to a little circle. We had even adopted various habits. We would go to the Danton in the morning because it was the only place that was open. Then we'd head for the Old Navy and the Mabillon, and we'd eat pasta (which was disgusting, by the way) at Moineau's, before spending the night at the Bac. We never went to the Flore or the Deux Magots. They were far too expensive for us. The Mabillon was already pricey compared to Moineau's. At Georges's in Rue des Canettes they would choose whom to admit, and it never included us. We'd often go to the café opposite the Lara Vincy Gallery, La Palette. But it's very different today. As indeed are most of the others. When we stayed a little too long without consuming anything, they'd soon make it clear that we were undesirable. The form of wandering that characterizes the dérive is intimately linked to psychogeography. I recall the tunnels mice used to make in the lawn, when I was young. And the tracks of the rabbits where I'd lay traps in Cornwall. You discover certain places in a city that you start to appreciate, because you are welcomed in a bar or because suddenly you feel better. This relates to the feeling you have in one place and not in another. As Debord put it so well somewhere in his writing, if you set off on a dérive in a good state of mind, you'll end up finding a good place. Yes, that's what it is, and I'd even say if you put me in an unknown town I will find the place where I should be.

I once got lost in Cologne and couldn't ask the way since I didn't speak German. But using a map of London, I quickly found Spoërri's restaurant and the address of George Brecht. And in fact that's what usually happened to me. I remember a night

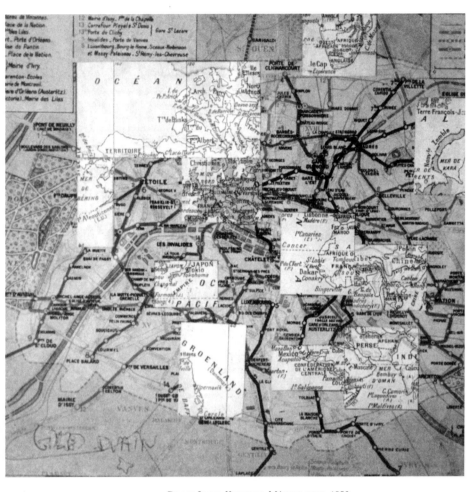

GILLES IVAIN, *UNTITLED*, MÉTAGRAPHIE, 1952

THE ISLAND OF LINOSA
PHOTO: RALPH RUMNEY

when I'd drunk a lot with a Swedish friend. We were at the junction of Rue des Canettes and Rue du Four. We were broke and had just been thrown out of our hotel. We were telling ourselves that we were absolutely fed up with this mess. And I said: "Let's split up. You choose whether to go left or right, and I'll go in the opposite direction, and we'll meet in New Delhi." That's what the dérive is—it's up to you to follow your own. I'd have to get there by hitching or God knows how. I set off and didn't get any further than Sicily, on a little island called Marettimo. Later, I got a letter from the Swede, full of recriminations, because the bastard had actually gone there. He'd arrived in New Delhi and hadn't found me at the American Express. I had intended to go there, but my steps had taken me elsewhere.

Often in life I've felt the need to take my distance from things. A few years later, I discovered the island of Linosa, a difficult place to reach because of frequent ferry strikes and bad weather. Linosa lies to the south of Sicily, practically in the Gulf of Sirte. A place where I've made several retreats of a year or two during my life. I've always felt entirely at ease among the four hundred inhabitants, regularly cut off from the world for long periods.

Some people have accused me of having a morbid love of solitude, but I would claim that what I found there was rather a small society on a human scale.

Was it this solitude that allowed you to paint?

I painted a great many pictures. I introduced figurative elements, like pricks and suns, painted words arranged on large sheets of brown paper. I take whatever colors come to hand. I don't say I am going to do a white painting or a red one, I simply say: "It's time I got back to work." I look for happily improbable color combinations, trusting to chance—a

GUY DEBORD, "ECOLOGY, PSYCHOGEOGRAPHY, AND TRANSFORMATION OF THE HUMAN MILIEU"
(UNPUBLISHED MANUSCRIPT, SIX PAGES)

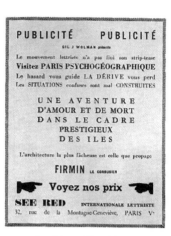
LES LÈVRES NUES, No. 7

serendipity like in Walpole's novel. But I'm not trying to be provocative: I think they are beautiful colors. It's true—there's shit brown, blue-violet, and there, you see, a touch of green. It isn't obvious, is it? And I use palette knives, art brushes, paint brushes, but I haven't the faintest idea how it works. I can look out of the window and see a whole heap of colors, but then I change them. The result may suggest a landscape, but it isn't one: it still works if you turn it upside down. Apart from the portraits.

I prepare my own canvases, with gesso and rabbit-skin paste. This makes them more solid, even if it's time-consuming. I mix my colors as I go along. When I start a painting I have no idea where I will go with it. So I apply the first brush stroke; the first suggests the second, and so on. In a funny kind of way the paintings paint themselves. Even though I have done highly studied works, I don't like the notion of the artist having complete mastery over his painting, instead of allowing it to evolve naturally. Which raises the question: how to stop? I can't answer it. I simply feel that something is finished. Otherwise, as in the *Unknown Masterpiece*, one would never stop.

It varies with me. I may take a few hours or a few days to do a painting, but never months.

Two things are in play in the result: one highly dynamic, which is the gaze penetrating the image, and one very static, which is the image itself, which varies according to light and so on, but remains essentially fixed.

Mondrian complains somewhere that everyone keeps going into raptures about his perfect static harmonies whereas what he wanted and believed he had done was to create compositions of dynamic equilibriums.

In my paintings I have motifs that may or may not be abstract—apart from the heads—and these are not laid down in advance, not planned; they've evolved as the image has developed.

I managed to sell a few paintings, and when I was short of cash I went back to London. I found myself in rather a difficult situation because I had left my canvases with someone who didn't want to give them back. Finally, I found a London patron who gave me £200 for some paintings. With this money I went to Italy and wound up in Trieste. It was there that I had my first exhibition, in 1955, in a café. It had a certain small success. I sold a painting which must have been three meters long. It was bought by a chap who wanted to decorate his office. Having some sense of humor, I asked if I could take a photo of him sitting in front of my painting. He agreed. He was as proud as can be. After that, I went to Milan, for Trieste was the end of the world, you didn't know whether it was Italian or Yugoslav. Go west, young man!

What was your impression of Milan at that time?

In one sense, Milan was like New York: modern, edgy, aggressive, very tough. I met several Italian artists, including the most important. They used to have a system that was popular in Milan: you could pay shopkeepers and restaurant owners with paintings. You gradually established a list of collectors. This wasn't easy because artists tried to keep their own collectors. Who could blame them? The only person who shared his knowledge was Fontana. He never stopped asking me why I hadn't tried approaching this person or that person. He was the most generous. But generosity wasn't common. In my experience, *artists*, the practitioners of artism, are the meanest and most anally retentive people I've ever met.

IF YOU WANT TO BE LOVED, LITTLE ONE, THEN YOU MUST LET YOURSELF BE KISSED BY. . . .

How did it go in Milan?

It went well for me. I had two or three exhibitions. The problem was that I was still without doubt the youngest and thus somewhat scorned by Crippa, Dova, and *tutti quanti*. But what the hell—I had quickly understood who they were. For sure, and it's a bit pretentious of me, but they were my inferiors. Milan saw itself as the true capital of Italy and still does today. At the time, there was an intellectual provincialism there, with regard to everything, which was very trying. I was young and perhaps aggressive. I didn't hold myself back. Crippa tried to kill me with his car one evening. Luckily, I jumped into a doorway, and the only thing he killed was his car. You see, it was an incredible atmosphere. And then I got together with the Apollinaire Gallery—a name that I rather liked—to organize an exhibition which was quite a success.

A solo exhibition?

Yes. Then I had another one with Mario Bionda, and I wrote this text which we both signed: *The Antiaesthetic Manifesto*. It infuriated everyone in Milan at the time, especially the painters and art critics.

You wrote it in English?

No, I wrote it directly in Italian. Then I got someone to correct the mistakes. Then Bionda got it published in *La Frustra*.

La Frustra *was a fascist periodical.*

Yes, but I didn't know that. Otherwise, I would not have allowed it to be published there. Within the art world it caused a bit of a fuss, a little stir in a rather closed circle. Then Klein came to exhibit at the Apollinaire Gallery. All his paintings that were the same size, the same color—unexpectedly, I liked them. I persuaded Fontana to buy one. Along with Klein, Manzoni, Baj, and Jorn, I was part of a sort of clique that was heavily frowned on by official Milanese artism. We used to meet in the Giamaica, a kind of local Moineau's. It hadn't taken me long to find it, any more than it had with Moineau's in Paris. It was the café of Milan's artists and "artists." We were completely against what I call provincialism, something I talked about in *The Antiaesthetic Manifesto*. I was scornful of most Italian painters, but Lucio Fontana—who was of Argentinian origin— was someone whose work I greatly respected. Baj, too, had a few flashes of talent, perhaps through the influence of Jorn.

But the only one I consider to be a real painter, poor man, died too young: Manzoni. He was doing

ADVERTISEMENT FOR RALPH RUMNEY'S EXHIBITION IN THE APOLLINAIRE GALLERY IN MILAN, 1957

We are against taste and we are
against antitaste. We have nothing to
do with mathematical research. We
know everything about the past and
everything about the future. We do
not want to convince anyone of anything. We do not want to make and
we do not want to see "beautiful"
paintings. Because we are convinced
that it is wrong to privilege a refine-
ment of materials following aesthetic
laws to the detriment of the "actuality"
of the painting. We believe that spatial
research is only valid when supported
by paintings. However, we condemn
the resurgence of a Futurism that is
all too predictable: Futurism was no
less "pastiche" just because it was
supported by a manifesto.
We believe that manifestos are a
necessary part of artists' activity. But
while we recognize their propaganda
value, we believe they are only justified when supported by paintings.
A painting is an object in itself and
not a decorative ornament. It is the
painting that creates the ambience
and not the ambience that determines
the painting. A painting is engendered
by inspiring forces; it is not composed
of discouraging forms.
Today we live in a world that is being
renewed. So it is useless to seek new
values; rather it is a matter of understanding that there is no real separation
between the painting of today and
the painting of the past.
The fundamental values of painting
are immutable. For a painting must be
appreciated in relation to what it tells
us today. Our only basis for judgment
lies within us and comes from our
environment.
RALPH RUMNEY, MARIO BIONDA

horrible paintings when I knew him. He was even
younger than me, a student. He did pastiches of
Reggiani. One evening when I was round at his
place I said to him: "If you want to be an artist you
won't do it by making paintings. You must live the
life of an artist. It is a practice, so that even your shit
should be a work of art." A little while later, he was
putting shit in tins! Later, when he made his white
canvases, I think he expanded the concept of the
monochrome. Because, say what you like, even if
Klein's blue monochromes were important, it was a
dead end. Manzoni found a way out that to the best
of my knowledge no one had the intelligence to
continue. He died even before he reached thirty.
One blinder too many: he drank himself to death.

Was it in Milan that you met Asger Jorn?

Yes, in 1956. Baj introduced me. He got me to translate his text on the Imaginist Bauhaus. No one
noticed that I was mischievous enough to translate
Imaginist Bauhaus as "Imaginary Bauhaus." Even
Asger hadn't spotted it until I told him. He roared
with laughter because in a sense it was right, if a little wicked. I'm anti-expressionist, but I liked
Asger's painting very much. I find he possesses a
kind of inventive genius that is entirely lacking in
Appel, Corneille, Alechinsky, and the rest—all
idiots, in my opinion.

Alechinsky turned up just before the end of Cobra.

More or less a couple of days before Cobra died. I heard
him many times recently on France-Culture because
there was an exhibition in Paris, and it was mediatized to
the limit. He was presenting himself as more or less the
founder of Cobra. Well, he didn't say that, but it was as
if it was his creation. Alechinsky has a style, an

approach, a tone, but it's always the same. He's someone who found something that worked and, instead of innovating, carried on repeating it over and over. There is never any change in the way the work is produced, in his approach, in the conception, or in the color. When I took Asger to London we went to an exhibition of Alechinsky or maybe it was Appel; it's the same thing. There was a typo in the exhibition catalog, a wrong date. It said that Alechinsky had started painting in 1752 or 1533, something like that. Asger nearly died laughing. He said: "Yes, that's him! He stopped painting a year later." Alechinsky is lithography endlessly repeated. That is what we call artism.

So let's talk about artism.

I think Michel Guet came up with the term. I found it in his writing. Some guy discovers a clever little idea, it goes down well in the market, and he repeats it forever. That's how I understand it. I find it can be usefully applied to everything that I consider false in the art market. When you find an idea, instead of exploiting it to death, the least you can do is to come up with another. What Michel Guet understood is that in the reductive, spectacular system of the art dealers, with artists as their accomplices, you have to stick with your one idea, become known through it, and acquire an international reputation through this single image. This kind of positioning, marketing as they call it today, was indispensable if you were to find a place in the art market. The merit of Michel Guet was that he found the right word for it, became its taxonomist.

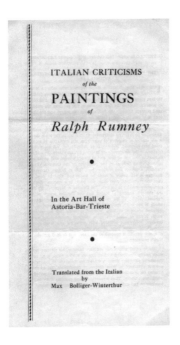

ITALIAN CRITICISMS
of the

PAINTINGS
of

Ralph Rumney

•

In the Art Hall of
Astoria-Bar-Trieste

•

Translated from the Italian
by
Max Bolliger-Winterthur

BOOKLET ON RALPH RUMNEY'S FIRST
EXHIBITION IN TRIESTE, 1955

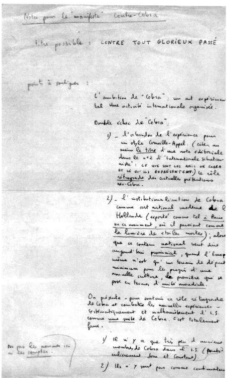

GUY DEBORD, "AGAINST COBRA"
(FIRST PAGE OF AN UNPUBLISHED
MANUSCRIPT OF TWO PAGES)

A little later, you participated in the exhibition of British Abstract Art.

Yes, that's right, in 1960. Lawrence Alloway and Robin Denny had invited me to participate. English abstract "artists" exhibited a series of very, very large paintings, around three meters in size. It was organized by the artists themselves, through some sort of association. I had painted three vast canvases. They've now disappeared. I had bought a grip and a stapler to stretch them out. I noticed something: among all these English artists I was the only one who knew how to stretch a canvas and who had the necessary tools.

You went around like a plumber, with your toolbox. . . .

Exactly. I had to stretch out canvases for a great many people. The paintings were not transportable. And often enough the frames weren't quite the right size. I had been horrified by the fact that they called the exhibition "Situations." They'd stolen and misused the term. I wrote them a letter telling them it would have been better to call it "Recorded Evidence." This obviously got a few people's backs up. There was a second exhibition called "Situations" the following year. I wasn't invited.

What do you know about Jorn's détourned paintings?

Baj, Jorn, and I used to go to the flea market on the outskirts of Milan where you could find various old daubs, bad paintings displayed by the poor. Someone said: "What if we altered them?" The results were fantastic. Baj was already making kinds of montages with generals and monsters, and maybe Jorn stole the idea of monsters. Or maybe it's the other way round. Who knows? It isn't important to know who was first.

There was an exhibition later at the Eugène Boucher Gallery with a text by Jorn entitled "Peintures Détournées" and an introduction by Jacques Prévert.

Exactly.

Piero Manzoni

To change the subject slightly, it seems that you beat Duchamp at chess?

Except that he let me win.

How did you meet him?

When I was a member of the Institute of Contemporary Art there was a conference in his honor, followed by a reception. It was very select gathering. Even the great English art critic, Lawrence Alloway, Penrose's deputy, wasn't invited. Roland Penrose, the director of the ICA, held the reception in his home. I knew or thought I knew everything there was to know about Duchamp from the books I'd read. He was my hero. So I went to see Penrose and told him: "I know that you are organizing an evening in honor of Duchamp, and I want to come." Penrose decided to let me in, and Alloway asked me to question Marcel Duchamp about Jackson Pollock. The place was packed: everyone wanted to meet Duchamp. I was fascinated by his work and by his mind. I went up to him and said: "I'm Ralph Rumney. Pegeen is my wife, and she told me to embrace you." With that, we kissed.

M
O
D
I
F
I
C
A
T
I
O
N
S

Détourned painting/ Aimed at the
general public, easy to understand./ Be
modern,/ collectors, museums./ If you
have some old paintings,/ don't despair./
Keep your souvenirs/ but détourn them/
so they suit the times./ Why reject the
old/ if you can modernize it/ with a few
brushstrokes?/ It will throw contemporary light/ on your old culture./ Be up
to date,/ and distinguished/ in one go./
Painting is finished/ So finish it off./
Détourn!/ Long live painting.
ASGER JORN

You didn't waste any time!

No, and from then on I monopolized poor Marcel.
He said to me: "Let's go into the next room." There
was a chessboard designed by Max Ernst. I had created a chess set that I preferred to Ernst's. It's long
since vanished off the face of the earth, but one of
my ambitions before I die is to find it again or recre-
ate it. Duchamp asked if I knew how to play chess
because then we could chat while we were playing.
As we played, he began laying little traps for me.
Then he let himself be beaten. I'm a very average
chess player. Chess isn't a game of intelligence but

of memory and calculation. It's like poker, like almost all the so-called games of chance that man has invented, totally stupid. If you can remember all you have to, you win. If you have a shaky memory, you lose. As I was leaving at the end of the evening I thought, shit, I forgot to talk to him about Jackson Pollock!

So chess, poker, casinos, they're all the same?

Yes. Moreover, I had invented a martingale. But don't forget that Duchamp had also found one. I didn't know that, but one day I invented mine. I used to play poker to survive in London. I demonstrated it to a painter friend and told him that I'd tested it on a roulette game, and it seemed to me to be unbeatable. I can't remember anymore exactly how it worked. It involved doubling stakes, of course, like all martingales. One evening, in some drinking den or other, we were playing poker, and my friend, who had also put it to the test, said: "Ralph has invented a martingale that I find unbeatable." He took out the paper on which it was explained. He said: "We each put ten pounds in the kitty, we send him to France so he can play in the casino, and we see how he gets on."

You went and you won?

I kept winning until they threw me out. I should have kept the piece of paper because my martingale worked. Let us say that it was the fruit of luck and necessity. Luck was on my side that night—because I only played for one night—but I took about a hundred times more cash than they'd staked, including travel costs and everything. Not bad!

MARCEL DUCHAMP

This was your scientific side!

If you like. But I believe that there must be a total fusion of art and science. Back in ancient Greece, arts were the praxis of philosophy. The split between them came in the Middle Ages, through the Church.

Among artists, who else do you think has brought together art and science?

Leonardo, Cellini, but there were so many. Today, there are very few. Kowalski, for sure, very impor-

RALPH RUMNEY WITH HIS CHESSBOARD
PHOTO: H. SHUNK

tant but unrecognized. And Marcel Duchamp. When I'm looking at one of his paintings I have to admit that I don't think it's very good. But when I imagine the brain that has conceived this work, I would say that I am in the presence of a brilliant mind, the greatest artist of the twentieth century. He was fascinated by photography, mathematics, and linguistics. Jules Marey's invention of chronophotography, which gave birth to cinema, impressed him deeply. So did the invention of the zoopraxinoscope by Muybridge, the pioneer of animated photography who recorded the different movements of a galloping horse. Duchamp's *Nude Descending a Staircase* can be compared to those series of pictures.

Duchamp had also been very struck by what could be seen, successively, through windows and mirrors. Perhaps this was a result of his encounter with Picabia. It was in 1913, I think, the year of the great turning point, of all the upheavals in art. You can make a history of art by tracing, if you like, a kind of evolution from Impressionism to Pointilism to Cubism, etc. All that seems straightforward. But what is interesting about Dada and Futurism is that they were totalities—that's what was new. There was a way of being, a way of living that was independent from the production of objects. In that resides the big break, the big return to basics. But that didn't just happen in the Café Voltaire. At the same time, for example, you had Malevitch or the Italian Futurists.

I don't see any contradiction between the Dada movement, Russian Futurism, and Italian Futurism. There were movements which at first were unaware of each other and which shook up all the basic assumptions in different parts of Europe.

Yes, and though I'm not an art historian, I would say that according to my own interpretation it began with people like Alfred Jarry, Raymond Roussel, and others. That is, it was something that passed by osmosis from the written to the plastic. It's an interpretation that every "artist" would challenge.

On the subject of the fusion between art and science I've mentioned Duchamp, but we should also talk about François Le Lionnais. If artists are cut off from science, scientists are also cut off from art. Completely cut off, poor things! We should help them to come back to us. They have one verifiable thought, which is: if you put a glass there, you will find it there later. If an artist puts a glass there and then finds it somewhere else, it's because someone has moved it or because he's forgotten where he's put it.

So Duchamp was working in this direction?

Yes, he was, and that included his interest in chess. In his pictorial research, he was aiming for an alliance with the sciences and mathematics. In an another field, there was a similar development in OuLiPo with Queneau and Perec. I found a lot of their linguistic experiments, like the lipograms, rather boring. What impressed me most, even

ETIENNE-JULES MAREY, *RUNNING*, 1883

ARTIST: n. and adj. practitioner of artism.
Works of art are the discharges of the artist.
The "artist" manufactures spectacular market commodities lacking any significance beyond their market value.
All the products of an artist are susceptible to recuperation and conversion to "artism."
The "artist" manufactures works which are already recuperated.
RALPH RUMNEY

83 | THE CONSUL

It is often said that art is a form of communication—a kind of paralanguage—and indeed, the shadow of semantics can be seen in our readings of paintings. With realism, the shadow deepens. The same goes for literature. When words are used in their "real" sense or read with realism, we enter the world of the word game, the spoonerism, the anagram, the palindrome, of paranomasia and chiasmus. In the same way, in painting we lose ourselves in the labyrinth of metaphors, anamorphosis, paramorphosis, not to mention isomorphosis, cryptomorphosis, the trompe l'oeil, Escher, Arcimboldo, etc. Art can be envisaged as the other side of the coin of solipsism. The paradox of the palindrome.

RALPH RUMNEY,
THE MAP IS NOT THE MEAL, 1984

though I never had the courage to verify it, was Perec's palindrome that extended over more than five thousand words. If anyone had told me such a thing existed, I'd never have believed them. The beginning and the end correspond, but faced with the task of reading the whole thing in both directions, my courage failed. Perec was a decent man, even though he cheated a bit in *The Disappearance*. These were all artists who focused on art and science as a totality, and managed to integrate this completely into their work. I consider myself as belonging far more to this current than to Cobra.

You added science and mathematics to your artistic development?

Yes. In 1964, I started working on a project that I called the International Institute for Arts and Technology. My idea was to create a center for work and study where artists and scientists would collaborate on the conception and realization of innovative projects, taking my inspiration from the Renaissance. Such an enterprise was only possible with enormous funds—I estimated a million dollars. To free ourselves of all constraints and external control, we had to finance ourselves. So I proposed that one thousand artists would contribute by each donating a painting worth a thousand dollars at the time. We would have to set up a kind of tontine in which the capital would consist of eleven thousand shares at one hundred dollars each; the first thousand shares would be allocated to the donor artists, and the rest would be sold to the public. Only the artists would have voting rights at shareholder meetings. This association of investors would last for twenty-one years, at the end of which the funds would be distributed among the survivors or their beneficiaries, the statutes having stipulated that the million dollars thus acquired will have been invested and the interest from this will have paid the salaries of a small permanent staff. I had obtained the agreement and guarantees of a large Wall Street company. The catalog of the thousand paintings would have been published by a reputable auctioneer, who would then have the right, twenty-one years later, to carry out the sale of the works. The works acquired would be loaned to museums in the artists' own countries during this period, thus avoiding storage and insurance costs.

The municipality of Venice, concerned at the time with the abandoned islands in the lagoon, was favorably disposed towards the idea of giving me one for the location of this institute in return for a symbolic rent. My proposal aroused great interest from the industrialists, universities, foundations, and artists I contacted. Three hundred artists had already agreed to participate. Sadly, the hazards of my personal life put an end to the project.

After my expulsion from the SI, my life became quite ordinary, or normal, I should say. I was too busy finding the money to enable my family to survive. I made paintings, oscillating between poverty and wealth. We moved back and forth between Venice and Paris.

When I heard that Pegeen knew Victor Brauner, I told her: "I adore that man!" And she replied: "We'll go and see him." I turned up beneath the viaduct at the back of the Gare de Montparnasse. Victor lived in one of the archways where he'd made himself a little nest. At least it was protected from the wind, but there was water running down the walls: it was sordid. Jacqueline, his wife, must have been a saint, to live in it. You know, Brauner had lost an eye. . . .

VICTOR BRAUNER
PHOTO: ANDRÉ GOMÈS

An accident with Oscar Dominguez. . . .

That's right, Dominguez. But Victor was so witty,
courteous, generous . . . he loved Pegeen, everyone
loved Pegeen. And he received me very warmly.
You see, I was a painter, therefore a colleague. . . . I
was shocked to see one of my heroes, this mythical
character, living in such conditions. Pegeen and I
were looking for a larger flat than the one on Rue du
Dragon. We went to look at a duplex in a new building on Boulevard Saint-Germain, and by coincidence Alexandre Iolas, whom Pegeen knew well,
turned up at the same time as we did. He had just
bought the ground floor of the building to house a
gallery. I spoke to him about Brauner, and Pegeen,
normally rather shy, supported me and proposed
that all three of us go to Victor's place straight away.
No sooner said than done. Six months later, Victor
had moved into a large and luxurious flat in Rue
Lepic, for Iolas had given him a contract. Victor and
Jacqueline were over the moon. There was a huge
room with a gallery where they received guests.
Victor proudly announced to anyone who cared to
listen that the room below would become a brothel.
His life was transformed. He had another place in
the north of France, and he set up his brothel in
Milan. To go there, he would walk down to Place
Blanche, jump in a taxi and say: "Driver, take me to
Milan." And since he was quite rich, he treated him-
self to girls in Milan to the point where it became a
bit of a scandal.

Why?

Because it was said that he went to bed with three
girls at once. And that got around, you know. It
wasn't acceptable to general morality at the time.
    Pegeen and I entertained a lot. One evening at
the end of the meal she said: "OK, I'm going to the

bathroom to kill myself." Which, of course, made everyone laugh, except me, for I knew that her suicidal tendencies were very real. This time she meant it. Before I got to her, she had swallowed a pack of Valium. Albert Diato and I spent the night making her sick and getting her to walk. Sadly, these events were all too frequent. One day, Peggy found her daughter in her bath, full of her blood. She phoned an ambulance. They rushed her to casualty. Once there, she was put in a corridor and left there. Her mother had already gone. She spent the whole night like that. It was her birthday. Long afterwards, Pegeen told me that she had let herself be sexually assaulted by one of the staff. I don't know if that's true, but anything can happen. In any case, she stayed in hospital for two or three days. Her mother never came to see her.

After another of Pegeen's suicide attempts, I phoned Max Ernst, who lived three blocks from us when we were in Rue du Dragon. I told him that Pegeen was in a bad way, that my financial situation was very precarious, and that it would be a good idea if she could be taken to the South, to get

PEGEEN BEING PHOTOGRAPHED BY RALPH
PHOTO: H. SHUNK

some sun, some beach, etc. Ernst sent his maid to verify the facts, as if he suspected I was trying to extort money from him. The negotiations took three days, then he gave us a little money and off we went. He realized himself that he had acted badly. He loved Pegeen and had often painted her: there are many well-known paintings by him where the nude woman is in fact Pegeen. He could have come round in person. . . .

Pegeen took alcohol and barbiturates, and you drank?

Yes, and I still drink, a victim of the Volstead Act, which introduced Prohibition in the United States in 1919. Pegeen's milieu, her mother and father, were part of that generation of American alcoholics from the 1920s. I would sometimes get pissed, but I wasn't used to the American martini system, where you got drunk before dinner. I took to it like a fish to gin. In the case of Pegeen, who took barbiturates and tranquilizers, the alcohol-medicine cocktail was toxic. I tried as far as I could to stop her taking one or the other. In theory, she agreed with me, but it caused her painful stress. One day, returning home in Paris, I didn't find her. In extreme distress, Pegeen had called her mother because I had forbidden her to combine alcohol with high-dosage Valium. I cut off her supply of tranquilizers.

A few days later, I got a call from a Swiss clinic. Fabrice, her elder son, had taken her there on the advice of Peggy. It was the beginning of the end. I managed to speak to her. She sounded desperate. She told me: "You must get me out of here. They are forcing me to drink and to start taking tranquilizers again. I can't bear any more." She told me she was going to escape, and we could meet up in Venice. I went there to find her at her mother's house. She was being looked after by Peggy's doc-

tor, a perfect bastard. He'd put her back on Valium. When I saw this, I really lost my temper with him. You know that with stuff like that it's very hard to stop once you're back into it. And she had practically stopped.

I don't want to give the impression that Pegeen was only a depressive woman or only tormented by her neuroses. She was an artist who lived her art and whose life was art, and as I've already said, there's a high price to pay for such integrity. Her paintings, especially the pastels, are very deceptive if you only look at the surface where, at first glance, there is nothing but light, color, and festivity. It's only after a deeper contemplation that you perceive the poignant beauty and anguish that her work breathes. Her work reflected her experience.

Peggy tried to separate us. She wanted to keep her in her palazzo, to which I was denied access. But Pegeen managed to escape. One evening, Peggy invited me to dinner. She offered me fifty thousand dollars in return for agreeing never to see her daughter again. I told her to go and fuck herself. When I told Pegeen, she said I was an idiot. She claimed I should have accepted and we could then have run off and enjoyed ourselves.

How did Peggy behave after you married her daughter?

I think Peggy did everything she could to destroy our relationship and to have control over her daughter. For Pegeen, the situation was unbearable. I've lost count of the number of times I saved her from suicide attempts. She was depressive, or rather, I would say, anguished. Pegeen's problem, in my opinion, was that she wanted a real relationship with her mother, but her mother was incapable of having human relationships or giving affection. Out in the social world, Peggy was witty and clever, chic and elegant, but at night she'd be up counting the slices of ham left in the fridge in case the maids had taken one too many.

Where did the family fortune come from?

The Guggenheim saga began in Montana, where one of the ancestors, a Jewish émigré who had escaped the pogroms in Switzerland or Austria, arrived and began peddling homemade medicinal ointments. They sold well, and he made quite a bit of money. One day a customer who couldn't pay him gave him a piece of land, instead, a hill which he soon established was more or less pure copper. That led to the Minnesota Mining and Manufacturing Company. It's the origin of a thing which exists to this day, 3M. He had a dozen sons, who became the Guggenheim Brothers, who made money out of oil, railways, strikebreaking, and other activities. Esso was them in the beginning. Their fortune was more than vast. Peggy is the daughter of one of the sons, one who in fact separated from the others. He took out his share of the businesses to throw himself into manufacturing lifts for the Eiffel Tower. They didn't work, and he was ruined. He was up to his eyes in debt. He tried to return to the United States on the *Titanic*, and we know how that ended. He managed to save his mistress, who escaped before it sank. She went to the Guggenheim Brothers and demanded that they pay her boyfriend's debts, to the great distress of his wife. They gave her a pension, and she lived comfortably to a great age on the Côte d'Azur. Peggy would visit her every year to see how soon she was likely to croak, for she would then get the pension. Peggy gave the impression of being rolling in money. That's a bit exaggerated, but she was certainly very well off, even though she was always complaining about being the poor Guggenheim.

What kind of relationship did you have with Pegeen?

Our relationship wasn't always simple, because it was very passionate, perhaps not very conventional. It's still a mystery, you know, how you can be very close to someone and be powerless to intervene in their personal tragedy. I saw myself then, and still see myself now, as someone who kept her alive. On the last occasion, I failed, you could say.

In February 1967, Jeanne Modigliani was in Venice. She phoned me because a mutual friend who was staying with her had disappeared a few days earlier, leaving all his stuff behind. I suggested she go to the police; she didn't want to and asked me to go for her. The police commissioner had one of my paintings on the wall behind his desk—a painting I'd given him to thank him for rescuing us, Restany and me, from some sordid setup in a red-light bar. To my astonishment, he asked me to state my identity. I did and explained the purpose of my visit. He asked me again to state my identity and kept this up every couple of minutes for a good quarter of an hour. He soon attained his purpose. I lost patience and asked him if he hadn't gone mad. Using the other cops as witnesses, he accused me of insulting a police officer and put me under arrest. I was handcuffed, photographed, and imprisoned.

The next morning, I was hurriedly condemned to expulsion from Italy. In court, I bumped into Jeanne's missing friend: he must have been tried for fraud. Handcuffs on my wrists, I was taken to the French border.

I got back to my place on the Quai de Bourbon at dawn, where I found Pegeen with the children—they had had to stay in Paris because of school while I was in Venice working on commissions. Understandably, Pegeen was devastated by the situation, which seemed to have closed the door to

Venice, thus preventing me from completing the work I'd been commissioned to do. She was convinced that what had happened to me had been engineered by her mother.

She had started drinking. Tired by the journey and my adventures with the police, I decided to go to bed quite early. She kissed me and wished me good night. She told me she'd sleep in the *chambre de bonne*, the spare room, and asked me to look after the kids in the morning, make them their breakfast, take them to school, and feed the cats.

Sandro woke up. I fed the children, sent Nicolo off to his school, and went with Sandro to his. When I got back, I realized that I'd forgotten to feed the cats. Pegeen had taken them with her. I discovered that the door to her room was locked. I knocked the key out on to a sheet of paper that I'd pushed under the door. I took the key and opened the door. Inside, I found Pegeen lying on the floor. I lifted her on to the bed. She was dead. The pathologist decided that she had committed suicide by taking sleeping tablets and whisky.

Peggy Guggenheim accused me of murder and of failing to assist a person in danger. I suspected that my mother-in-law was going to cause me some problems.

The staircase was crowded with journalists, so I couldn't leave the flat. So I got out on the roof and then went down through the next-door loft. I immediately telephoned Eleonora Marmori, who was a journalist for *Il Giorno*. I told her all the facts in the presence of Fabrice, the eldest son of Pegeen and Hélion. This account appeared in the paper the next day, and every time I was collared by a journalist I would tell him to go and read the article in *Il Giorno*.

PAGE FROM *IL GIORNO* (8 MARCH 1967) REPORTING PEGEEN'S DEATH: "AN OVERDOSE OF SLEEPING PILLS, A TRAGIC MISTAKE"

Dear Ralph, Peggy succeeded in raising the suspicion that you might have killed Pegeen. This rumor has returned to you twenty years on, as you've returned to Venice. You weren't expecting this at all: it's opened old wounds. I am very grateful to Fabrice Hélion who has recounted to us an interview he had with his grandmother. I remember the exact words. "Do you really believe Ralph killed Pegeen?" "Of course not!"
SYLVIE METTETAL

I was kept away from the children. I didn't have the right to see Sandro, for I had asked a friend to pick him up from school and to take him to a half-sister of Pegeen. I never saw him again until he reached the age of majority. Often during those miserable years, I regretted that I hadn't sent him to stay with my friends. Still, I tried with every legal means to get him back, but I quickly realized that I had nothing that could stand up to Peggy's money. I was disarmed. Worse, they were going to hand the boy over to psychiatric specialists—I preferred to give up.

I had the surprise of learning that an unlikely number of people had made defamatory statements about me. Lawyers had put pressure on Hélion's children to bear witness against me, saying I used to beat up my wife or whatever they wanted. They warned me. But there were far too many people who made statements, including very many whom I'd never met. One friend, Dixie Nimmo, told me that one day on the terrace outside the Gentilhommière, at Saint-Michel, he was approached and offered ten thousand dollars if he would testify against me. My reaction was pretty much the same as Pegeen's some six months earlier when Peggy wanted to buy me for fifty thousand dollars.

Peggy had me followed by private detectives and had a microphone hidden in my telephone. I discovered it and sold it. She wanted to prove that I had a mistress and that this was the cause of Pegeen's suicide. They followed me everywhere. So I walked a lot. I would go from the Ile Saint-Louis to Montmartre, then back to Montparnasse. I wore out the private detectives by making them go on dérives without knowing it. But I still had to find a way to avoid going to jail.

Is that how you came to give art classes at Félix Guattari's experimental clinic?

I had a very good friend called Albert Diato, a potter. He said to me: "Listen, Ralph, the only way to be protected is to be hospitalized." I took him up on the idea because prison doesn't have a great appeal. So he took me to the clinic at La Borde and explained my case to Félix Guattari, who was a friend of his. I didn't know Félix, but he told me: "Here no one can touch you. You can stay. And you can give classes in drawing or painting." So I moved into the clinic. There was a disused greenhouse, where I set up my studio. Actually, there was an old man there, a long-term patient, who had already made it his home. He hadn't spoken a word to anyone for years. He had decided the greenhouse was his domain and sat there typing all day long. That was his thing. Most people would have said: "OK, he's a crazy old man—don't bother him." For he gave me typed texts to make it clear that I was disturbing him in his home. But I felt that in fact he was disturbing me in mine. In any case, we had to put up with each other. So, not having a typewriter myself, I spoke to him. I told him: "Félix has said that I should work here and that if people want to learn about painting they can come, too." My tactic wasn't to invite people to come but simply to say: "Look, if you want to paint, there's this place you can use, with all the materials you need, and so on." And slowly, one by one, people started to turn up. This poor guy got more and more annoyed. But the result was that one day he spoke to me. It was the first time anyone had heard him speak for I don't know how many years. In the world of psychiatry, it seems that this incident is well known.

ALBERT DIATO

At the university of Kent in Canterbury, one day in 1976 I saw a poster announcing that the department of European Studies had invited Mr. Ralph Rumney to give a talk on the legacy of the Situationist International. The name rang a bell. Hadn't this man once actually been a member of the SI? I looked him up in my battered copy of Christopher Gray's *Leaving the Twentieth Century* (these were still the preindustrial days of Situationist historiography, and there wasn't much else). There he was, number four on the list of members. Section: Italian. Nationality: English. Expulsion: March 1958. An early renegade. I consulted with one or two friends. We didn't know much, but we knew recuperation when we saw it. A *university lecture* on the SI! Outrage! (Younger readers at universities where many otherwise worthless academics now build their careers around such things and lectures on the SI are a dime a dozen may find this hard to imagine.) Fragmentary knowledge of Strasbourg or the Sorbonne inflamed us: we must act. A tract was penned; an intervention planned.

The lecture room, unfortunately, was far from packed. In fact, apart from a few polite academics and a handful of the kind of dutiful students who attend everything, there was only us. A mild-mannered professor, a specialist in *Tel Quel*, gave the introduction. Then, late, in came Rumney. He didn't look like a recuperator. In fact, he was strikingly handsome, slightly resembling the young Artaud. He didn't look happy, either. I cannot remember how he began his talk, probably because I was so nervous at the thought of the historically necessary task we had to perform. I forget, too, which one of us stood up to denounce him. It might well have been me; I was the tallest. "You are," I suggested awkwardly but

Which goes to show that if you are condescending to people, you perpetuate the state they're in. You said: "I don't see why this jerk should have more right to be here than I have." And he said to himself: "But this jerk isn't behaving towards me at all like the other jerks."

In this instance, my approach was more effective than that of the shrinks at La Borde. But when all's said and done, I didn't even do it on purpose.

How long did you stay at La Borde?

I often went back there because of my painting classes. I'd go there two or three times a week. And in my role as fake patient, I stayed there a week or so. I think Guattari set up this clinic to try out his ideas about psychiatry. I met quite a few people there, and my impression is that in the end he established this place for the down-and-outs of the world and for American deserters. It was a refuge from which I benefited a bit. I remember another story. At that time I had a Renault 2CV that I used to drive to the clinic. One day, I left it down there for a few weeks because I'd gone back to Paris with Félix. I'd advised him to buy some welding materials for a young man who'd been a welder before going into the clinic. I told him he could make some sculptures. When I went back to pick up my car, it wasn't there. The young guy had broken it into pieces to make a sculpture, something I thought was rather brilliant. I appreciated that very much.

You stayed a fugitive afterwards?

No. It was decided there were no grounds for prosecution. But you know, throughout my life I've always been wandering, never stayed in the same place. I went to London because I was at last free to leave Paris. I'd been promised a job in an art school, but it never materialized. So once again I found myself practically homeless. I saw some adverts for bilingual switchboard operators. I was taken on as a bilingual operator in a telephone exchange on night shifts. That was what I did in 1968. You know, the fact of being in perpetual movement is perhaps another reason why I've been in some ways close to the Beat Generation. The dérive was an element we had in common.

So you left Paris?

I was compelled to stay there until it was decided there were no grounds for prosecution because of Peggy Guggenheim's accusation. Once I had the chance to leave, I took it. And indeed there wasn't much to keep me in Paris. Peggy's lawyers had taken away my son. My financial situation was quite disastrous; I was forced to beg from friends. After my stint in the telephone exchange, I found a job as an illustrator for a history magazine. I was a picture consultant! That lasted for a while, and then, through my usual ineptitude for employment, I got myself fired.

I wandered here and there for a few years. I don't know how long exactly, as I have a bad memory for dates.

When I returned to Paris in 1970, I began to make it a habit to get drunk in the Rosebud in Montparnasse. I met a chap who was dead drunk when we found ourselves in the street together at four in the morning. He asked me to take him to the Maison de la Radio because he had to prepare the morning news broadcast. He had difficulty standing, so I put him in a taxi, and off we went. I was pretty far gone myself. He led me into the scriptwriters' room and fell asleep. I slapped him on

heroically, "betraying your own past by reducing a revolutionary movement to one more academic topic within a bourgeois university. You are being paid by the specialists of the spectacle to recuperate the only. . . ." Luckily, Ralph interrupted me at this point. "Yes, I was just thinking more or less the same thing myself," he said. "And it wouldn't be so bad if they were paying me properly. But, you know, I'm only getting £15 for this nonsense. Is there a bar round here where we can get a drink?" The meeting broke up in mild disarray, and we headed for the bar. I suspect we paid for the drinks.
Malcolm Imrie

Ralph's finances seemed always to alternate between penury and an almost ridiculous abundance. One day you'd visit him in a squalid room in Neal Street, in a house he shared with people who were more or less tramps; the next you'd meet him in Harry's Bar in Venice or at the opening of a Max Ernst exhibition in Paris, on the arm of Pegeen Vail, whom he married soon afterwards. It seemed to me that he accepted poverty with more equanimity than wealth.
GUY ATKINS

the cheeks to wake him, and he asked me to prepare the morning news bulletin for him. News wires were coming out of various ticker-tape machines, I had to put them in order. When I finished, I woke him up, and he read what I'd written on the radio. This wasn't a major national station like France Inter but a little program broadcast to francophone countries in Africa. Apparently, it was fine. He remained eternally grateful, and whenever we were together I'd get blind drunk.

He advised me to look for work in the English-language section and recommended me to Sturge Moore, who was a kind of living legend. He was the one who broadcast the appeal of 18 June 1940 when he was at the BBC. He gave me a kind of oral exam and asked me to prepare a news bulletin in the order that seemed best to me. We made a recording. He told me it didn't work because my voice was gloomy and boring. So he sent me to the other section, two floors above. I was lost in all those circular corridors when someone called my name: "Ralph! What are you doing here?" It was a friend, Gerald Cazaubon, whom I hadn't seen for six years. We'd met in a nightclub, La Grande Séverine, when Memphis Slim was playing there. I told him I was looking for a job. "I'll find you one!" he exclaimed. And that's what he did. I worked for the radio for three or four years.

Whom did you meet there?

The most important encounter was with François Le Lionnais. He was the science and culture consultant for ORTF (French national radio and television), and he came to find me. It seems that he liked some of my broadcasts. He, too, was a chess fanatic, a friend of Duchamp and a member of OuLiPo. He published several books on it. He was in rather poor health because he'd been in Bergen-Belsen. As he was a scientist, they made him work on what were called "flying bombs," the V1s and V2s, which the Germans used to attack London. He told me that his job was to make sure the gyroscopes in them were properly calibrated. Obviously, he damaged them as much as he could, which had the rather unfortunate result that neither the Germans nor the English knew where the flying bombs were going to come down. For the English, it was frustrating because they couldn't calculate where to intercept them. He thought he was doing the right thing, but the results were somewhat mixed.

FRANÇOIS LE LIONNAIS IN HIS OFFICE
IN BOULOGNE, 1976
PHOTO: OULIPO ARCHIVES

At the end of the war, when the camp guards disappeared and the Americans arrived, he left with a whole band of people, and they occupied a town where the Germans had suddenly become extremely humble and obedient. From the Bürgermeister down, everyone was at their service. They had the best houses, the best food, the best clothes, just about anything that was left in the town. And in all the confusion that reigned at the time, he enjoyed considerable autonomy, So he took the job and the house of the Bürgermeister and ran things in his own way. In the end, it didn't last very long, but from what he told me it was a little bit of revenge that he greatly enjoyed.

Did you see your companions from the days of Letterism again?

I often saw François Dufrêne, Gil Wolman, and Jean-Louis Brau. Brau certainly had talent, but he always seemed to me more like a character from Céline than anything else.

He moved to the right.

Yes, and he'd been a mercenary. At an opening for I can't remember whom, at the Lara Vincy Gallery, I ran into him. We shook hands, and I said to him: "I'm pleased to see you again." And I added, "Give your daughter a kiss from me when you go home." He punched me in the face. What I didn't know was that his daughter had just killed herself. A gaffe, but how was I to know? It wasn't exactly headline news in *France-Soir.*

Brau had been married to Eliane. Did you know her?

Yes, very well. She was vulgar, but she had her charms. Like many others, for that matter. Among the people I saw again in the sixties there was Robert Filiou, one of the most significant artists I've got to know. I saw Jacques de la Villeglé, too, but less frequently, at gallery openings. And I had a high esteem for Raymond Hains and his torn posters.

In fact, this technique had already been dreamt up by Léo Malet during his Surrealist phase. It was Wolman who pointed this out to me. It was obvious that it had been exploited, or rediscovered, by Dufrêne, by Gil, by Rotella, by Raymond Hains himself, and many others. The dérive, psychogeography, it's all there in Malet's crime novels.

Not bad for one man, when you think of the place those things occupied for the Letterists and Situationists.

Poor Malet, when I was at ORTF I wanted to do a program about him. He was already old. All I can claim is that I spoke to him on the telephone, and he more or less told me to take a walk.

We do what we can.

Yes! Anyway, out of all the poster artists, it was François Dufrêne to whom I felt closest.

I've heard it said that "Ralph and François were made to be together. They never stopped clowning around, never stopped laughing."

Yes, and in a sense the biggest joke was on one of my return visits from Venice around 1980. I'd phoned François and made an appointment for the next day. But in the meantime, he died. The following day, it was almost dawn, I went to his funeral in the Montparnasse cemetery. And afterwards I went with a few of his pals to La Coupole to have a drink to console us for our loss. The result: I got a serious case of pneumonia. It nearly killed me, too. When I was back in Venice, I still hadn't recovered from the pneumonia or his death. I began looking at the posters in the city with a fresh eye. I had often helped François tear down posters in Paris. As I had a car, it was easier to carry them around. But I'd never seen this as an activity that was relevant to me. I consider that François Dufrêne is the best poster artist I have known, certainly more interesting than Rotella, who pretends to have invented everything.

FRANÇOIS DUFRÊNE, *JAPPE JAP*, 1958

Jorn did a bit of poster work, too.

Indeed, but, you know, in that milieu there was also a kind of jealousy about who did things first. Some people even altered the dates to put themselves first. But not François and not Wolman, either.

It is a tradition in art to pay homage to those who have gone before, and it seemed to me almost my duty to make a kind of monument to François

RALPH RUMNEY, *TORN POSTER*

Dufrêne. How should I do it? I told myself, OK, I will be a temporary poster artist. I made I don't know how many, a dozen, a score. Twenty-five years later, I think they stand the test of time. It's easy to like what one makes; otherwise, you wouldn't make it. I exhibited these posters in a restaurant in Venice because, as I've told you already, I've always been a bit scornful of art galleries.

In Venice specifically or in general?

In general, everywhere. And then exhibiting in restaurants has always been a tradition in Italy. In Trieste, Florence, Milan. . . . In Venice, as every-where else, there were hierarchies of artists, jealousies, and a sort of little gang I knew where those who were excluded came together. They weren't all good painters, but there were two or three interesting ones.

I had the idea, partly psychogeographical, of publishing a map of Venice that would indicate all the restaurants. The plan was that each artist should pick his own restaurant. Get the owner's permission and organize a little show as he liked. It was open to all artists; there were no criteria for excluding anyone. In the end, there were fourteen artists. Whoever found a restaurant for his works would be included on the map, which would be given out to tourists and to clients before the exhibition. The idea was also to get people to walk around so they would get to know Venice a bit better. The participating restaurants weren't on the city's usual tourist trails. Most of them were only known to the Venetians who lived in the areas. The project was carried out, but without me, oddly.

You didn't find a restaurant to exhibit in?

Yes, I did. But I had framed a whole lot of photos of breasts. I turned up with my Polaroids, which I'd called *Breasts*. The proprietor had really done up his restaurant for the event. It had never been so chic. Until then, it was a bit of a dive. OK, I'd hung everything up, it all looked fine, and the proprietor was very happy. Then the cook arrived. She took a quick look and went into the kitchen without saying hello or anything. A few minutes later she reemerged, livid, with a big knife in her hand and a look that was, shall we say, menacing. She shouted that if it wasn't all taken down immediately, she'd walk out. And it was evident that she planned to do a bit of damage before leaving. The proprietor tried to calm her. I quickly realized that he risked getting his throat cut or his stomach opened. So I took my photos down and left. And indeed I was the only painter in the group who didn't get an exhibition.

Soon, collage will be performed without scissors, razor blades, paste, etc., in short, without any of the tools currently needed. Leaving behind the tables and portfolios of artists, it will take its place on the walls of cities, an infinite field for the production of poetry. Never before has the popular saying which suggests that poets can "eat bricks" [or "live on thin air"—*Trans.*] acquired the concrete meaning which knowledge of poetry's lithophagous power can bring. No longer is it possible to believe that the one and only goal of the awful, solitary, sanctimonious, and interchangeable poster artists is to exalt the virtues of this or that commercial product. . . . With or without the consent of these people, the posters that have fallen asleep on their feet will awaken and poetry will devour the walls.
LÉO MALET, 1942

PROGRAM OF THE "IN BOCCA
ALL'ARTE" EXHIBITION, VENICE, 1984

How did the project work out?

It aroused a certain polemic in the local paper for
two or three weeks. The paper's art critic was out-
raged by the development. He thought it threat-
ened the trade of the art dealers. He asked what
restaurants would do if art dealers sold meals and
wine. He added that it was against the law and
encouraged the sale of forgeries. I replied with a
long letter saying that it was ridiculous to suggest
that artists would exhibit forgeries of their own
works in these restaurants, especially as all the participating artists were more or less unknown. Most
forgeries are bought in galleries. I mentioned
Giorgio de Chirico in this respect, and I said that if
galleries started running restaurants they might
learn that the true laws of commerce don't include
duping customers and suppliers. Throughout the
exhibitions, I continued to receive indignant letters
from the galleries. Which kept me amused.

After such a success, did you repeat the experience?

I created an association for local artists in Manosque,
without any selection procedure. They could show
their works in the shopwindows of the old town.
The first year, it was a huge success, not from the
point of view of sales but in terms of the affective
ambience in Manosque: the shopkeepers were
happy and so were the artists. It was the grandson of
the Venice restaurant project, you see.

There was no judging of quality. Everyone
brought their paintings—they were distributed, and
each person got his own thing in a shop. It had been
agreed with the shopkeepers that the association
would decide what would go in which window. Most
kept to the agreement, but a few hid the paintings
behind the stuff they were selling. Out of season, it

created an unusual coming and going in the old town. We did it for a second year, adding a huge canvas in the square in front of the town hall and providing material so that everyone could have a go at painting.

Then I fell ill. There was a bit of trouble on the little committee which ran the project—some people wanted to take it over; I'd never exercised any control, just put forward various proposals which were generally accepted. Now I no longer have any contact with it. As far as I can understand there is now a selection procedure, and it is more or less only women who exhibit. They had the idea of exhibiting in banks. Yes, well, perhaps women have been ignored for too long, but even so this kind of sexism is beyond me. Where was I?

Talking about the ORTF and Wolman.

Yes, and I remember him taking me to an exhibition at the Grand Palais. A bizarre story. In the end, it seems to me that most of my life has been bizarre. A woman asked Gil to introduce me to her. Nothing could be simpler. We lived together for a year or two. She lived by the Seine in the fifteenth arrondissement, which was very practical while I was working for the radio. It began very well, and then she began to find me a pain. She had a son, and she would take the piss out of me in front of him. So there I was, I don't know, on the eighteenth or twentieth floor of this place, which was actually quite stressful as I suffer from vertigo. One afternoon or evening, I took off, leaving everything there. I even left my car in the lot, you know. But, well, I'd had enough.

The Polaroid is a particularly pertinent tool because the negative, here, is immanent. It is all done with mirrors. Although the sexual attributes of the female are the oldest raw material for the artist that we know, my intention here is not at all erotic. Still, I admit that the semiotic power of these ideographs is stronger than that of a still life of a café table with newspaper, bottle, and guitar. Let us avoid metonymy. Photographs and molds of breasts: these tits will never give milk. As Dufrêne often said: "That's art there." RALPH RUMNEY, *BREASTS*, 1984

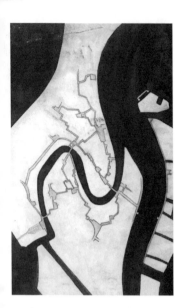

ROAD MAP FOR THE "IN BOCCA
ALL'ARTE" EXHIBITION

You lived with her and didn't know where you would go?

Exactly. I'm sure I had enough on me for a hotel room. So as all the hotels I remembered from before were around Rue du Four, Rue des Ciseaux, Rue des Canettes, that's where I headed, because at the time it wasn't expensive, and I felt at home there. I must have had a drink at the Flore, and then I walked around Saint-Germain. I noticed there was an opening at La Hune. So I said to myself, good, maybe I'll meet someone I know there. I went in, and indeed there were people I knew. Afterwards, there was a party at the home of Claude Clavel, the painter whose exhibition it was, and there was Michèle Bernstein. . . .

Whom you hadn't set eyes on for twenty years.

Yes.

You were twenty at the time, and now you were nearly forty.

Yes. And we fell into each others' arms, just like that, so happy to see each other again. We started telling each other jokes, couldn't stop making each other laugh. I ended up in Rue du Temple, at Michèle's place, in fact. Bit by bit, I moved in with her. You see how small the world is. I went and got my car back. I was very fond of it—it was a '53 Traction. It wasn't worth then what it would be today. Actually, it's the only car in my life that I've ever sold for more than I paid for it. I went to Poland in it and to England, Italy, Greece. They're tough, those old cars.

How was it with Michèle?

Very good. There was the occasional blow-up—I was even quite violent sometimes. I don't remember why anymore, but one evening when we were watching TV something annoyed me or I was drunk as well, for sure, and I threw the TV set at the wall. It exploded.

Speaking of TV, they were building the Beaubourg just behind our place at that time. The building work drove all the rats and mice out of the drains. One mouse moved in with us. It would sit on the floor and apparently watch television. We rather liked that, you know. Michèle isn't the kind of person who will faint when she sees a mouse, as many women do, apparently. And then this mouse had the bad manners to invite all its pals, to the extent that we were really invaded, infested. Michèle wanted to call in the rodent disposal people. I said, no, absolutely not, we must find a cat. I thought we could get one from a local concierge. But I didn't know Michèle. She goes off and looks through the cat Larousse or whatever. We got a Russian blue, three or four months old. On the day it arrived it killed a mouse, and that was the end of the problem.

Had Michèle Bernstein divorced Guy Debord?

Yes, long before. And I think she wanted us to get married so she could acquire English citizenship. It's something I never understood, but at the end of the day we are all entitled to our whims. From my point of view, I could have become French, which would perhaps have allowed me to get a staff job at ORTF, instead of being a mere freelance. My view was that marriage would eventually be necessary if we had children, but OK, if she thought that would be good for us now, I couldn't see any problem. It was touching.

GIL WOLMAN, ANTHEA ALLEY, AND
RALPH RUMNEY IN SALISBURY
PHOTO: MICHÈLE BERNSTEIN

And so you agreed.

I couldn't have cared less whether we were married
or not. If you live with someone, you have obliga-
tions either way. It also gives you certain vague
rights; at least, it normally does. We pissed ourselves
laughing after the wedding when we had to go to
the British consulate in Paris. Michèle had to take
an oath of fidelity to the Queen. We were trying not
to offend the consul, but it was such a ridiculous
oath, it meant nothing to us. She received her passport, and that was the end of it.

In principle, it should have been a reciprocal
arrangement, and I had the right to become a
French citizen. But to do that I would have had to
be registered for social security, get a residence permit, and God knows what. At least one didn't have
to swear loyalty to Giscard. Anyway, as I already had
some sort of legal status, I didn't bother. Then I met
Michèle's father.

What was he like?

Formidable, wonderful. If I had a quarter of his erudition, I'd consider myself rich. He was a walking
encyclopedia. If you asked him any question, he
could answer it and find you the relevant book. He
was a bookseller with an international reputation. In
my opinion, booksellers don't usually know what
they've got. He knew everything. I don't know how
he had found the time, but I got the impression he'd
read everything. I know that even today when
Michèle needs to know something, she calls her
father. Me, I call Michèle. In most cases, when I
have some doubt about a matter of opinion or a date
or a memory, it is Michèle I ask. I phoned her the
other day because something was nagging in my
memory. I remembered a piece of graffiti I'd seen

for the first time in Paris in the 1950s which said: "Free Henri Martin." I really couldn't remember who he was, and, curious as I am, I called Michèle. She replied: "I remember that, but you posed me a tough one there." A rare event!

When you were married to Michèle, did you see Debord again?

Yes, once.

What happened?

I expressed the wish to see Guy again if he would meet me. We went to his place in Rue Saint-Martin. It wasn't a bad flat. I met Alice, his second wife. They were both charming and immediately opened a bottle of Antinori, a very fine Chianti, almost as good as Fagiolino Chianti, which I only knew by repute. And then Guy began to do something rather curious. He spoke to me about Michèle like a lord and master, as if he still had some kind of propri-etary right over her and I was a passing fling. Michèle, who was sitting next to him, had clearly had enough of this, and got up to come and sit by me. It was a bit of theater, to counter Guy's behav-ior. You could say that it was a bit stupid as a response, but, well, it was on the spur of the moment. And then we ate, and towards the end of the meal I began talking about the problems I was having with my papers and residence permit. It was perhaps not the best thing to say, but I asked Guy if he knew anyone who could help me obtain these papers, saying: "It could perhaps assist me if you could introduce me to anyone halfway decent that you've encountered at the Prefecture during your dealings with the legal system." He went off the rails. He shouted: "Get out!" And he threw us out of the flat. It had given him a pretext to lose his temper. In his head, by asking him that I was taking him for a cop and that he would not tolerate. It was the last time I saw him.

And how did Michèle Bernstein react?

I spoke to her on the phone recently about the incident. She has a slightly different memory of it to mine. She credited me with having used my English sense of humor. "You were perfect." I see her as a pillar of support, someone I can always rely on. She will never tolerate anything that annoys her. But her sense of humor is a joy. One evening, during our time in Canterbury where I taught art, I was a bit worried because one of my students had barricaded himself inside a kind of shelter he'd made out of his canvases. He refused to come out or to communicate. Despite my superiors' wanting to call the police and the student psychiatric services, I got an agreement that we would do nothing until the next morning on the grounds that he might see things differently after a night's sleep. Michèle had told me the solution was simple: I only had to give him Melville's *Bartleby* to read and everything would sort itself out during the day. Which is exactly what happened. I don't think Michèle ever knew how to become a Debordist. She kept her intellectual independence, which is not an easy thing, especially with someone like Guy. She had a classical education to begin with, which was insufficient for someone of her intelligence. I think Guy brought her some of the rest and made her understand how to learn other things. And she knew, maybe thanks to Guy, how to free herself intellectually, even from him.

To me, she is the most Situationist of all. She was the one in Cosio who picked everyone up on the fact that one does not say "Situationism" but

RALPH RUMNEY,
UNTITLED DRAWING, 1955

"Situationist," because when it becomes an "-ism" chances are that it will turn into an ideology, a sect, a religion. She would surely deny this, but I had the impression that she had a certain authority over Guy. She used it extremely sparingly but at the right moments. She knew how to rein him in when he slipped into the worst kind of exaggerations. Between Guy and Michèle there was a serious, lasting complicity when they were together and even afterwards. Guy's sudden rejections of people could sometimes be paranoid. Michèle tempered this side to his character. In any case, the whole history of the SI is full of excesses. And Guy will always remain an enigma, for too many of the pro-situs, post-situs, and others who knew him have interests to defend. We observe with dismay the birth of extravagant cults, bizarre sects, and fundamentalists as barmy as they are bigoted. I have heard recently that some "Orwellians" have seen fit to remove Gianfranco Sanguinetti's signature from a new edition of the book he coauthored with Debord, *Theses on the Situationist International and Its Time*. It's probably not true, but rumors often presage infamies. There will soon be piles of nonpersons.

It seems Guy wanted to remain an enigma, but I think I can discern in his writings the traces of extreme caprices, justified by the similarly shameless hubris of the man I had the honor to know for a certain time and who did more than any other person of our age to unmask and dismantle the spectacular stage on which everyone struts and frets his hour.

There's another question that's more profound and also banal: how does one become Guy Debord? I would modestly suggest that the answer is in his life, in the real honesty that lay behind the masks he used to make the unbearable livable. I greatly hope that the various biographies now in preparation

I am not someone who corrects himself.
GUY DEBORD, 1992

won't spare their readers from making the effort necessary to understand that his blemishes were as important as the panegyrics.

You say that the history of the SI is full of excesses, but you, too, are a man of excess.

Obviously. But to be an artist is to be excessive. It's a ridiculous way to behave in the world today. Especially to be an artist in the sense I understand it. When I officially quit painting I still continued to live my life like a work of art. It was, it's always been, my way of being. The word "dandy" has one meaning in English, another in French. I have never entirely understood its French meaning, but I think it could come down to behaving like an artist.

Does the excess you're talking about also concern alcohol? I've noticed that most people around the Letterists and the SI drank a lot.

I won't make any apologies for all that. There's a tradition of alcohol in French literature which doesn't exist in English literature. You have Rimbaud, Baudelaire, Lautréamont. . . . In English literature you have De Quincey and his *Confessions of an English Opium Eater*. And there's Malcolm Lowry's *Under the Volcano*. Indeed, my sobriquet or pseudonym at the time was "the Consul," after the principal character in the novel. I didn't choose it myself, but I find it very amusing. When I was young I drank enough to go mad. Now, after a rather difficult period, I drink with the moderation of the extremist.

Does alcohol remove inhibitions?

Yes, it's the Prozac of artists.

Alcohol has a relationship to sexuality and also to creativity.

Let me quote Rumi: "Pour the wine so that, like an angry drunkard, I shall breach the portal of the eternal prison." But that takes us back to the Beat Generation. In fact, those I knew all took drugs or drank.

Like Dylan Thomas, whom I once met. It was in the Mandrake Club, a bar in Soho. I was having a drink there with a friend, Ricky, when he suddenly exclaimed: "Oh, my God, there's Dylan Thomas!" I couldn't see any problem. I went over to him and told him that my friend was an admirer of his work and would like to meet him. In his inimitable voice, Dylan replied: "As long as he's not a cunt, you can introduce me to him." So Ricky steps forward and says: "I, too, am a poet." Anticipating Dylan's reaction, I quickly ejected my companion with a kick up the arse.

With the Beat writers I also tried magic mushrooms, but didn't find the results very interesting. Brau, on the other hand, was very interested in such things. He even wrote a book on the subject. I just gave it a go, because I'll try anything once.

So the vital strength of his spirit won through, and he made his way far outside the flaming walls of the world and ranged over the measureless whole, both in mind and spirit.
LUCRETIUS, *DE RERUM NATURA*

There was another Situationist known for using drugs, Trocchi.

Yes, I knew him when he ran the review *Merlin*, a magazine of the Anglo-intellectual expat scene in Paris. He was kind and courteous with me. He put me up. But there was no friendship between us. Because, well, I'm addicted to cigarettes and alcohol, but that's not the same as other drugs. They cut you off from the world. At the end of the day, I scarcely knew him. But when he had those problems in New York, I tried to help him, as we all did.

What drugs did he take?

Coke. At least, I think so. I never asked him. Coke
or heroin. We would smoke marijuana and put away
liters of wine, but. . . . For a long time, I used
amphetamines. I've taken psilocybin, acid, hash.
Not mescaline, because I've never come across any.
I've never touched heroin, but I've tried almost all
the other classics.

Cocaine?

Yes. And if I could find some coca seeds, I would try
to grow some on the terrace. For a very simple reason: the Peruvians and the Maya used to chew it to
help with breathing. And as I have respiratory problems, it's not the derivative of coca that I want, it's
the leaves, so I can chew them. I don't know if it
would grow in the Lower Alps, but it would be an
amusing idea if it worked. I've had a blocked nose
all my life. Occasionally, it clears. In the beginning,
the reason for coca, or the reason it was cultivated,
was to help the natives of those regions to tolerate
the form of apnea caused by the high altitudes at
which they lived. In my case, it's not because I live
at a high altitude but because of smoking: I also suffer from a form of apnea that is called emphysema.
And if I could find something that would help a bit,
especially something so ancient, not to mention
organic. . . .

Ralph Rumney in the 1980s
Photo: François-Xavier Emery

No problem with destroying yourself, as long as you do it with something organic!

Ah, well. To go back to where we were before, the consumption of drugs is a very ancient practice. It goes back to shamanism, to Sumerian rituals, to the ancient Hebrews, and to pre-Doric Greece. Originally, drugs were the property of the intermediaries between men and gods. The vulgarization of their attributes of power gives the poor a spectacular illusion of subversion. Power tries to regulate the usage of drugs through the spectacle, just as it has already done in the fields of culture and sexuality, which become threatening when they get out of control.

When one is prepared to try anything, it makes a great difference to meetings with other people. But drink and drugs are two different things.

We're all drug addicts. You smoke your beedies, I smoke Gitanes. The trouble is that it becomes addictive.

Perhaps there is also excess in the interest you bring to eroticism?

I've already said that sexuality becomes subversive when it frees itself from controls. Eroticism is the creative aspect of sexuality and thus its disturbing side. Personally, I've tried to break the taboo employed by the spectacle to render pornographic any too-realist representation of the consequences of the temptation of Eve. I use photos and molds as recorded evidence. Just as I use the phrase of Alfred Korzybski's, "the map is not the territory," to stress that between representation and reality we enter the forbidden zone of fantasy. Symmetry, terrifying symmetry as Blake put it, often appears in my work through the body. Even if what fascinates me in bodies is precisely the way that a buttock or a breast is asymmetrical. Bodies are both symmetrical and asymmetrical at the same time. The problem of beauty is a thorny one. It is not one of my ambitions to make beautiful paintings; I don't feel at all concerned by aesthetics. But I'm not trying to produce ugly ones, either. Moreover, even ugliness can be beautiful. Most of Bacon's paintings are absolutely ugly, but by his perseverance he taught us how to find them beautiful.

But since we're coming to the end of these interviews, there's something I want to make more precise, on the subject of memory.

There are facts, realities that probably existed, memories. When you tell anecdotes you end up believing that what you have embroidered is the truth. Besides, realities are transformed by memory, or one simply forgets some things. Any witness, in my opinion, is always subject to doubt and, therefore, suspect. I've tried to be truthful and sincere. I've tried my best to be, in Rousseau's sense, as clear and truthful as possible. But I believe that you will adapt the facts that mark your life to things you can live with. This is true of everyone, and it's probably genetic. I don't think I'm an exception to the rule. Memory must then be treated with caution. Witnesses must be treated with caution.

We live things and just by virtue of living them, we don't live them in the same way. And when we recount them, forty, almost fifty years later, time has obviously done its work . . .

. . . and everyone wants to look good in history. I'm not claiming that what I've told is the true story. It is my solipsistic impression of history.

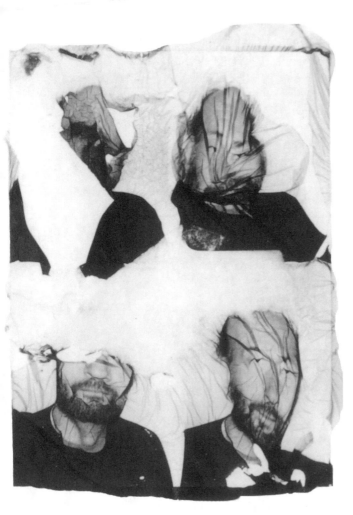

RALPH RUMNEY, *THE NEW ME / LE MOI NOUVEAU*, 1994

Our hope was always to change the world. That pretension is now defunct. You only have to read *The Society of the Spectacle* and *Comments on the Society of the Spectacle*.

It is rather the world which is going to change man's very nature, and the role of those who yesterday sought to change the world will become critical if humanity can come to want to survive fully and passionately the cataclysmic disintegration of the integrated spectacle.

The first, premonitory signs were already apparent back in Cosio, along with our clumsy outline of strategies to remedy it. It was agreed that every agono-ludic action has as its final goal to qualify the affective ambience: thus the plastic arts when used as part of this effort become an aspect of universal psychogeography. In Ravenna, or in Assisi, before all the cathedrals started to crumble away, the decoration was supposed to affect your behavior, modify the affective environment in the cathedral. For me, that is a key. Then painting with an easel was invented . . . and I paint with an easel. I still don't possess a basilica . . . I need to paint just to put paintings on my wall. For my own environment.

"In a classless society," we can read, "there will be no more painters but rather Situationists who, among other things, make paintings." But in 1962 these outlines of a strategy were abandoned. Analysis in depth was subordinated to the exigencies of the spectacular. It was a vital development, but instead of allowing the techniques already sketched out to evolve, it contributed to their being progressively occulted in the face of the obsessive, explosive development of the integrated spectacle, even though its implosion is ineluctable once it has reached critical mass.

And the pioneers are as lost as Hansel and Gretel in the forest.

It was a mistake to neglect the agon in the search for the ludic. But Huizinga isn't the only reference point for those who at least know enough of Van Vogt (even if some are still unaware of Korzybski), Philip K. Dick, and Clifford Simak, as well as the Old Testament, the *Iliad* and the *Odyssey*, to guide them. Later, there came the researches of Chomsky, Jaynes, Pinker, Kamal Salibi, and many others who illuminated the history of the last global revolution.

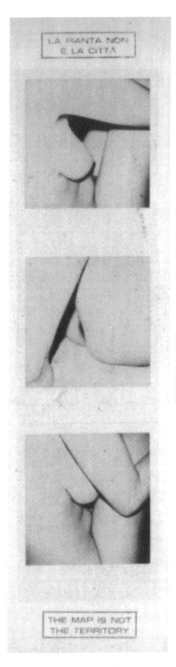

The Map Is Not the Territory

Certum est pars veri. / Certainty is only a part of the truth.
GIAMBATTISTA VICO

Here we can see that solipsism coincides with pure realism, if it is strictly thought out. The I of solipsism shrinks to an extensionless point and what remains is the reality co-ordinate with it.
LUDWIG WITTGENSTEIN,
NOTEBOOKS 1914–1916
(trans. G.E.M. Anscombe, New York: Harper & Bros., 1961)

Linguistic analysis is the essential tool if we want to understand the disintegration of self-awareness which will be the consequence of the impending implosion of the real. Though analysis of this is only now taking its first faltering steps, we are fortunate enough to have at our disposal enough witnesses of the only useful precedent to enable us to formulate similarly apt strategies in order to face the future. Like the *aoidoi* and other artists who clumsily helped our ancestors to find metaphors for the real voices of their gods when those gods remained silent.

We could say, then, that the first truly revolutionary act was the creation of metaphor. An eminently artistic creation.

As St. John said: "In the beginning was the Word, and the Word was with God, and the Word was God."

These interviews were recorded in Cosio d'Arroscia and Manosque between July 1998 and August 1999.

The author and the publishers would like to thank the following: Marcel Benabou, Michèle Bernstein, the town library of Cremona, Véronique Bourgeois, Miriam Bridenne, François-Xavier Emery, Jane England, François Escaig, Héloïse Esquié, Nathalie Fontaine, Yves Hélias, Malcolm Imrie, Bernard Kops, Barnaby Lankaster Owen, Eric Lang, Pauline Langlois, Fabienne Lesage, Fabiola Mancinelli, Sylvie Mettetal, Francesco Milo, Valérie Mréjen, Gabriele Muzio, M. Rapelli, Francine Rolland-Diato, Sandro Rumney, Philippe Siauve, Piero Simondo, Valeria Solazzo, Laurence Tacou-Rumney, Jasia Reichardt, Elene Verrone, Liliane Vinci.

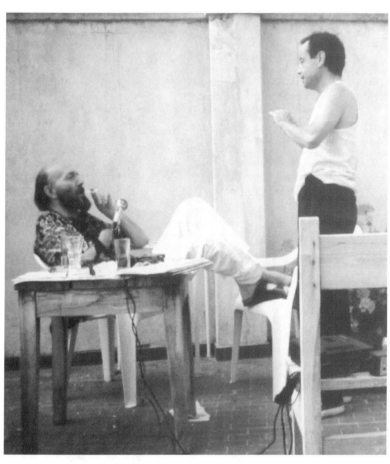

RALPH RUMNEY AND GÉRARD BERRÉBY IN COSIO D'ARROSCIA, JULY 1998
PHOTO: PAULINE LANGLOIS

Ralph Rumney died on 6 March 2002 at his home in Manosque in Provence. For some weeks before that he had been receiving treatment for cancer in hospital in Marseille. He was buried in Montparnasse cemetery in Paris on 9 March, his funeral attended by some of the people he talks about in *The Consul*, including Michèle Bernstein, Jacqueline de Jong, his son, Sandro, and his companion during these last years, Sylvie Mettetal.

I was there, too. I'd been fortunate enough to know Ralph for more than twenty years, ever since the first, ridiculous, encounter I briefly describe in this book. In the last few months I spent a long time chatting with him on the phone (bed-bound for the last year or more, Ralph loved to talk), occasionally about this translation. I delivered it late— and by the time I sent him the draft he was too ill to read more than the first few pages. He made a couple of corrections and no doubt would have made more—to my rendition of his words, that is, not to the substance of a book with which he'd been very pleased. Gérard Berréby, his interviewer, and his publisher in France, was one of his closest friends and had helped him a great deal during his illness. As had another good friend, the writer Alan Woods, who tragically died just as he was completing his own, superb, book on Ralph, *The Map Is Not the Territory*. Alan, of course, interviewed Ralph in English; Gérard in French. Ralph spoke French just was well as English. Still, it always seemed a bizarre enterprise to be translating the edited transcripts of French interviews with him into his native language. He could have rewritten it in English himself, I suppose, but even if he hadn't been ill, he had better things to do with his time. So he asked me to do it. I hope he'd have been happy with the results. I made the last corrections to the proofs a fortnight after his funeral, close enough to be able to recall precisely his voice in all our last conversations. Somewhere in this book, Ralph tells

of how he failed to get a job in the English-language section of ORTF because his voice was "gloomy and boring." It was never that, but was instead a deep, sonorous, rather upper-class English drawl. Precious little of that beautiful voice will have survived translation. But I would like to think that some of the other qualities that made Ralph such an inspiring man will still be found here: his acute intelligence, boundless curiosity, and vast erudition, his dry humor, and most of all his constitutional spirit of revolt. He says of Guy Debord that no one in our age did more to "unmask and dismantle the spectacular stage on which everyone struts and frets his hour." Maybe. All I know is that Ralph did his bit on that score, throughout his nomadic and inventive life. He was an avid listener to the BBC World Service and in the last months in particular the news brought him little cheer. The new century, he told me, certainly hadn't got off to a great start. I know I'm not alone in believing he embodied many of the more hopeful aspects of the last one.

Too bad he didn't see this little book. Too bad he didn't see the first publication of his photo story, *The Leaning Tower of Venice*, just published in France, some forty-five years after Guy Debord used its late delivery as a pretext for expelling him from the SI. And too bad he died before I'd been dumb enough to get a classical scholar to search for the Latin verse on page 8. Pseudo-Panoramitain, indeed. After his funeral there was a gathering at the flat of his son Sandro, the walls hung with paintings by Pegeen and Ralph. One of Ralph's included a "self-portrait," a montage of a glass surrounded by green packs of Celtique cigarettes, Ralph's favorite brand before they were banned for being too strong even by French standards. As people were finally starting to leave, a sudden gust of wind flung open the French windows with a bang. "It's Ralph," said Sandro, "come to get the last of the wine."

MALCOLM IMRIE

10. July. 02   HAI   12.95   85310